# Sherborne
and
# Castleton

## Abbey, Town & School
*Rodney Legg*

HALSGROVE

First published in Great Britain in 2004

DEDICATION

*To Colin Graham
who took many of the photographs*

British Library Cataloguing-in-Publication Data
A CIP record for this title is available from the British Library

ISBN 1 84114 240 9

HALSGROVE

Halsgrove House
Lower Moor Way
Tiverton, Devon EX16 6SS
Tel: 01884 243242
Fax: 01884 243325
email: sales@halsgrove.com
website: www.halsgrove.co.uk

Frontispiece: *Victorian print of the Conduit with railings, and the Abbey, westwards from Long Street.*

Printed and bound in Great Britain by CPI Bath Press, Bath

# Contents

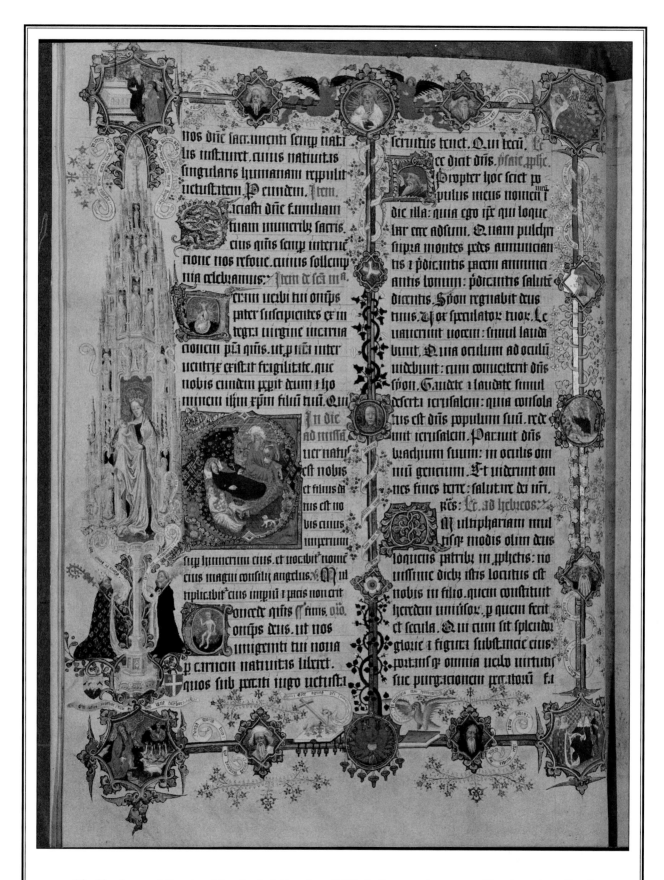

*The* Sherborne Missal, *a Mass book dating from 1400, is the most important illuminated medieval manuscript in the British Isles.*

# *Acknowledgements*

❧

From 1970 there is just one name synonymous with Sherborne and photography. Colin Graham of *Dorset County Magazine* was my cameraman until he moved to the other side of the world, to New South Wales, departing after a last exhausting bash in 1985. Subsequent photography has been down to me, also coming over the hill from a cottage near Sigwells, in tandem with making historical notes. Some date back to childhood research. Verbal contributions came from policeman Victor Swatridge and then teacher Gerald Pitman, affectionately known as 'Fossil' to his pupils, with updatings from Julia Crabb.

These days I generally do my own typesetting but I have been spoilt by an offer from former Fleet Street telegraphist Colin Leach from Charlton Horethorne. He now waters Sherborne's floral displays for Superplants – plus me in the Old Inn at Holton – but was delighted to have the chance to resume his old trade.

My other pleasant surprise was that Global Challenge participant Naomi Cudmore, my editor at Halsgrove, adapted and adopted a presentation very different from her usual tried and tested formula. I had originally produced conventional chapters on subjects such as Sherborne Abbey, Sherborne Castle and Sherborne School but found they became as repetitious as they sound, with the continuity spoilt by enforced returns to the Middle Ages. So we re-worked the text into a chronological format and then interspersed it with photographic sections where the emphasis is on individual buildings and streets.

Personal research has been augmented by recourse to the following books which have been on my table, seldom gathering dust, throughout a dry summer and wet winter in 2003:

Densham, W. and Ogle, J. *The Story of the Congregational Churches of Dorset*, Bournemouth, 1899.

Digby, Lettice. *My Ancestors: Being the History of the Digby and Strutt Families*, London, 1928.

Fowler, Joseph. *The Stones of Sherborne Abbey*, Sherborne, 1938.

Goodden, Cecil P. *The Story of the Sherborne Pageant*, Sherborne, 1905.

Gourlay, A.B. *A History of Sherborne School*, Winchester, 1951, and 2nd edition, Sherborne, 1971.

Hodges, Andrew. *Alan Turing: The Enigma*, London, 1983.

McKay, S.G. *Fosters: The Story of a Dorset School*, Dorchester, 1975.

Marsden, Frederick. *Sherborne Mill from Silks to Glass*, Sherborne, 1980.

Pitman, Gerald. *Sherborne Observed*, Sherborne, 1983.

Powys, Littleton C. *The Joy of It*, London, 1937. *Still the Joy of It*, London, 1956.

Riley, Lieutenant-Colonel L.P. *The History of the Sherborne School Cadet Force*, Sherborne, 1988.

Royal Commission on Historical Monuments. *Dorset, Volume One (West)*, London, 1952, plus Addendum, 1975.

Whitlock, Dorothy, editor. *The Anglo-Saxon Chronicle: A Revised Translation*, London, 1961.

Wildman, W.B. *Life of S. Aldhelm: First Bishop of Sherborne*, London and Sherborne, 1905.

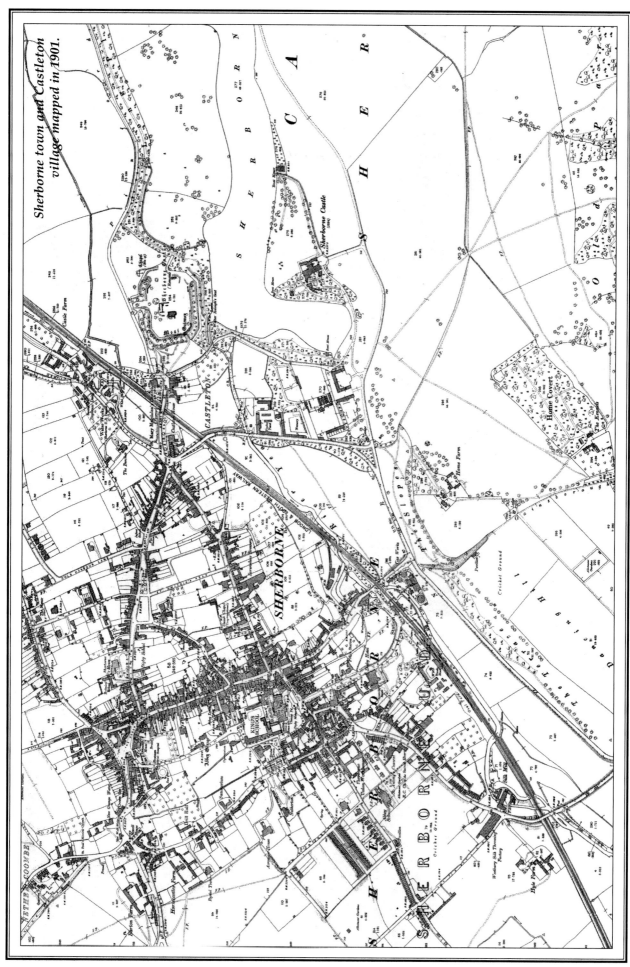

Sherborne town and Castleton village mapped in 1901.

# Introduction

Gold is the colour of Sherborne stone and there is a rich history to match. The seminal year was AD705, by which time Sherborne had the earliest cathedral in the West Country, and it remains Dorset's principal ecclesiastical town. The Anglo-Saxon cathedral evolved into Sherborne Abbey, now the Parish Church, which equals Corfe Castle in status – architecturally and historically – as joint first winner of the accolade for the most important building in the county.

The *Sherborne Missal*, written by Benedictine scribe John Whas and illustrated by the Dominican illuminator John Siferwas, dates from between 1396 and 1406, and is the finest medieval manuscript in the land. Having survived the closure of Sherborne Abbey it was taken to France, then bought by the Duke of Northumberland, and is now one of the principal treasures of the British Library.

Just across the parish line, at Castleton, the town has its own pair of castles. The first was created as a bishop's palace and the replacement built by Queen Elizabeth's favourite mariner, Sir Walter Raleigh. He lost his head, as well as Sherborne, and the next great name to arrive on the scene was Prince William of Orange who established his headquarters at Sherborne Castle, while en route to becoming King William III in the Glorious Revolution of 1688–89.

Around it, during the following century, the Digby family commissioned landscape gardener Lancelot 'Capability' Brown and architect Robert Adam to create parkland gems. They include a seat on the spot beloved by poet Alexander Pope.

Sherborne School has shared the Abbey complex since the reign of Henry VIII. Snow 'deep and crisp and even' inspired an old Shirburnian to pen the familiar line in the carol 'Good King Wenceslas'. This book tells the story of both town and gown. Contributions from old Shirburnians in the fields of war, science and literature punctuate English life and culture. They are also abundant in the wider context of the British Empire. One unique ten-year-old, who arrived at Sherborne in 1858, already held a combat medal. It had been awarded the previous year, after the Indian Mutiny, for his heroism during the siege of Lucknow.

The town, its scholars, and forces based locally made sacrifices in winning the Second World War. Bombing, almost all of it within a few minutes on a single afternoon, caused devastation on a scale unprecedented for a small country town. Alan Turing was the ex-Sherborne pupil who did as much as anyone in saving other places from the same experience by breaking the enemy's Enigma codes. A company of American Engineers, clearing up after a mine-laying exercise, were killed in Sherborne Park. Sherborne School's notable Victoria Cross was for the gallantry at Arnhem that was immortalised in the film *A Bridge Too Far*. Industrially, by developing glass-fibre products, the town contributed to technological advancements that are now taken for granted.

These days, many of the positive elements remain in place, with Sherborne still captivating visitors from Sherborn, Massachusetts. It lives up to their expectations of an archetypal village. That's their word.

Being inherently closer to an old English village, rather than a modern British town, has saved Sherborne as the place we love. Survivals more than offset what has been lost to the ravages of time. Museum Sherborne it may appear, as an exhibit in theme-park Dorset, but the town also has a vibrant present. The two come together in the historic Pack Monday Fair which still touches the spirit of the place.

*Edwardian ladies cycling west beside Robert Brine's tin-plate workshop* (right) *and Childs' Cycle Works, with Morley Read's grocery store ahead* (centre) *and the sign of the Castle Hotel opposite* (left).

*Valley cottage at Coombe Farm, where the body of Frederick Bryant was found, leading to his wife Charlotte being convicted of murder and hanged in 1935.*

**The ancient hollow way of a medieval road (centre), turning southwards towards Limekiln Farm, seen from the causeway of the present A352.**

# One
## ❧
# *Prehistoric Sherborne*

There remains a question mark over what has been claimed as the earliest Sherborne artefact. Although the 'Sherborne bone' has been authenticated as coming from the Pleistocene period, when Palaeolithic peoples came out of the caves on to what was still frozen tundra towards the end of the last ice age, its engraving of a wild horse has not been universally accepted as a piece of prehistoric art. According to William Johnson Sollas, Professor of Geology and Palaeontology at Oxford University, it did not date from 15000BC but was 'a clumsy forgery' of a bone found at Creswell Gorge, Derbyshire, in 1875. Both featured the head and forequarters of an animal similar to the species *Equus prezewalskii* from Mongolia.

The Sherborne bone – a semi-fossilised rib bone from just such a wild horse – was brought to Sherborne School and handed to science master Elliot Steel in October 1911. Two new boys from Abbeylands House, Arnold Cortesi and Philip Groves, described how they found it among quarry debris beside one of the old workings between Nethercombe and Clatcombe. The spot, beside a gully scoured by melt waters as the permafrost eased, would have been ideal for a rock shelter. The object had been authenticated by Arthur Smith Woodward of the Geology Department at the British Museum, president of the Geological Society, who gave a lecture on it in 1914. He drew attention to the teeth of mammoth and rhinoceros from the same era having been found further down the same valley.

After the First World War, though before the debunking of the notorious Piltdown forgeries caused a reappraisal of all such finds, doubt was cast on the carved bone from Sherborne. C.J. Bayzard, visiting Sherborne from Oxford, said that boys had admitted to him that it was 'faked as a practical joke such as delight the hearts of boys of fifteen.'

Cortesi, who retained an interest in archaeology on returning to Italy, insisted that it was genuine. The doubters pointed out that older boys could have planted it there for them to find. Groves could no longer be grilled about the matter as he had been killed at Arras in 1917. His mother did her best to defend his reputation. The defence rested on the fact that both were very young to have pulled off such a hoax, and unlikely to have done so at that time, as they had been at Sherborne less than a month. Elliot Steel and Sir Arthur Smith Woodward, as he had become, continued to believe in the authenticity of the object.

The remainder of Sherborne's prehistory comes from millennia later after the land had been put under cultivation. Lynwood Farm tenant Stephen Shutter told land agent E.A. Rawlence, at the Digby Estate offices, of his discovery of 'a hearth' exposed in the quarry on Low's Hill (Ordnance Survey map reference ST 610 161). An excavation in August 1915 revealed a late-Bronze-Age cinerary urn with bones and flint flakes. Christopher Biss from Coombe, who was present at the dig, pointed out that there were other circles – apparently showing the sites of huts or burials – visible in the fields above. Joseph Fowler went searching for them, without success, a generation later. With the coming of mechanised agriculture the light soils of the Bridport sands had become prime arable land.

*Outline of a wild horse, scratched on a Palaeolithic bone, said to have been found at Coombe.*

Thousands of prehistoric artefacts from around the Sherborne area were given to Dorset County Museum in Dorchester by Mrs Lucy Thorogood. They were amassed by her father, Charles Bean, who was the surveyor of Sherborne Urban District Council until his retirement in 1957. He came to Sherborne in 1925 and died in the town on 15 July 1983. For more than half a century he walked the fields, as an amateur archaeologist, picking up worked flints, pottery and pieces of carved stone. Each was accompanied by its map reference and a sketch showing the find spot. He also recorded the humps and hollows of previously unknown earthworks.

Museum curator Roger Peers described how 'literally hundreds of thousands of items' had been packed into hundreds of boxes that were filling his reserve collection store at Revd John White's Rectory in Dorchester. It was second only to Mr and Mrs Jack Skyrme's bygone collection in being the largest ever given to the museum.

Bean himself described 'the most notable series of flints' as those coming from fields around Silverlake Farm. He also identified the field names of the stony yellowish plots on surface beds of the inferior oolite a mile west of Sherborne. More than 200 flakes and cores, four fragments of Neolithic celts (stone chisels), numerous end scrapers and small round 'thumb-scrapers', and three early-Bronze-Age barbed and tanged arrowheads pointed to occupation from between 3000 and 1500BC.

I shall give Ordnance Survey six-figure map references for these locations and follow the same practice for other out-of-town locations as the book proceeds. Bean's most productive fields, from west to east, were an unnamed enclosure (ST 604 161), followed by Short Hound (ST 605 156) and Long Hound (ST 607 159). Next came Upper Clanfield (ST 608 157) and Lower Clanfield (ST 610 158) and Upper Louse Hill (ST 611 161) and Lower Louse Hill (ST 612 159). Then there was Home Field (ST 609 155), Poor Field (ST 611 153), Gravel Pit (ST 613 156), Lord's Bush (ST 614 157) and Bob's Ground (ST 618 158). Having been ploughed, these were ideal for field walking, but the settlement areas probably extended further east and also lie under the pasture of registered common land towards Lenthay Road (ST 620 154).

Excavations by Exeter Archaeology ahead of house building on Foster's Field, a former school sports ground north of Newland at Tinney's Lane (ST 643 170), revealed an extensive pottery-making area at the turn of the millennium. A total of 13,591 potsherds date in the main from 1000 to 800BC in the late-Bronze Age and are ascribed to the culture snappily named 'the Post Deverel-Rimbury tradition' from other type-sites in Dorset. More pottery of this period has been found in Sherborne than anywhere else in the land apart from Runnymede Bridge across the River Thames. Another 1,274 ceramic objects, mainly cylindrical with pierced holes and usually described as loom weights, were also recovered from Foster's Field. Refractory fabrics of the type associated with crucibles indicated that metalworking was also carried out.

Firings seem to have been carried out in shallow circular depressions with a mixture of straw, ash wood and gorse faggots. Pits and post-holes revealed charred Celtic beans, of the species *Vicia faba*, found in their thousands along with grains of wheat and barley, and occasionally oats. No huts or houses were found. So the big unanswered question is the location of the associated settlement. In all liklihood it has already been built over.

**Left:** *Bastioned earthwork, immediately west of the Old Castle ditch, appears to have been added during the Civil War.*

**Main:** *Lenthay Common, the town's former racecourse, back as pasture after wartime ploughing.*

## Two

### Roman Times

The rich agricultural lands of north-west Dorset supported a series of Romano-British villa estates. An extensive set of buildings was on Lenthay Green in Castleton parish. This villa site lies at the western end of Lenthay Road, just over the railway line – on the south side – between it and the River Yeo near Darkhole Farm (ST 624 153). Walls and floors were discovered in 1836 and a mosaic floor was removed and reset in the Dairy House at Sherborne Castle. The centrepiece depicts a naked Apollo playing the cithara with Marsyas holding two flutes as he prances in front of him.

Traces of its robbed east walls were followed by Charles Bean, during the hot summers of 1947 and 1949, when they 'showed in ripening corn' running up to the railway fence, east of the level crossing.

There was also a cluster of Roman buildings on the north side of the River Yeo to the east of the town, at Castleton, in meadows beside Pinford Lane north-east of the Old Castle (ST 654 170). The foundations of walls and cobbled courtyards extend northwards into the valley and are covered by a 15-inch layer of clay which indicates that it was flooded through the post-Roman period. Around these outlines, Charles Bean found the lesser marks of an oval enclosure, with numerous late-Iron-Age finds including a Durotrigic silver stater and a bronze Aucissa-type brooch. There was also Iron-Age pottery, including a rim and shoulder preserving impressed fingerprints, among fragments of bone in the soil of the roots of a tree that had been blown over on the hillside to the south.

The Roman buildings revealed quantities of de-luxe Samian pottery from Gaul, plus Cologne ware, and a spread of coins from Hadrian in AD120 through to Theodosius in AD390. Chunks of pastel-painted plaster from the walls indicated a place of villa-like status. Charles Bean also recorded 'traces of burning' from the time of its demise. The shapes of various rectangular Roman rooms and buildings were mapped in 1956 and dated to between AD138 and AD180 by coins of Antoninus Pius and Marcus Aurelius.

Farm labourers told Bean of 'bakehouses' which he thought were corn-drying kilns. After the war he discovered and excavated a T-shaped structure in the Long Plantation (ST 654 169) above Pinford Lane. On returning to the site, after the Southern Gas Board had put a trench for a trunk main along the whole length of Pinford Lane in 1957, he changed his mind and declared it to be the hypocaust furnace for an underground heating system. The remains of a significant second-century building was covered by

quantities of third-century New Forest pottery and other rubbish, as also were three more walls and yards to the west, where a coin of Nero was found in 1941.

Samian ware and fragments of Roman-British pottery, plus a scatter of roofing tiles, have been found near the spring to the north-east of Blackmarsh Farm (ST 652 180). There was also Romano-British settlement debris around Dymor (ST 631 187), near the spring above Sandford Orcas Road, with sherds of Samian pottery and coins from AD270 to AD337. 'Brooches, burnt areas, and the usual debris of a hut settlement,' were found beneath the strip lynchets of a medieval terraced field. Down the valley, a late-Roman coin of Constantine was found when Clatcombe House (ST 632 191) was built. From centuries earlier, a Roman Republican-period coin was dug up in the garden behind, after the Second World War.

On the other side of Castleton parish, both north and south of the railway line east of Bedmill Copse (ST 610 147), Charles Bean found wattle-and-daub buildings of a Romano-British settlement. Once again there was imported Samian pottery, plus later New Forest pottery, and the coins ranged from AD222 to AD383. Wartime ploughing revealed burials, close to the surface, including a skeleton with what appeared to be 'an iron spiral toe ring'. South-eastwards, in peaty deposits towards the River Yeo, 'a few flint scrapers and arrowheads and a segmental bead were exposed by the plough.'

Ploughing west of Almhouse Wood (ST 625 145), in 1955, exposed a scatter of coarser Romano-British pottery. Charles Bean then came across a similar spread of fragments north of West Lane (ST 665 157). He judged from the location and terrain that the nearby outcrops of flaggy-sandstones had been worked for roofing slates. The oolitic hills towards Milborne Port also provided building stone.

From there, at Goathill (ST 671 178), courtesy of the continuation of gas-main-trench digging, Bean found himself in another intriguing hole. A layer of burnt soil was followed by broken Samian ware and a third-century coin. Amongst the pottery, 4ft below ground level, he found a quantity of small rounded seeds. These were identified by Miss J.M. Thurston of Rothamsted Experimental Station as those of the pea *Pisum sativum*. A proud Bean was told that his pulses were only the fourth confirmed find of peas from a Roman site in the British Isles with the others being Wookey Hole, Silchester and Caerwent. No one told Sir Harry Godwin, however, so Mr Bean's peas were absent from Godwin's second edition of

*Apollo naked and playing the cithara, with a double-fluted Marsyas prancing in front of him, on the mosaic from Lenthay Roman Villa that was removed in 1836 and reset in the Dairy House at Sherborne Castle.*

the *History of the British Flora* when it was revised in 1975.

Chance finds of coins in Sherborne town include one of Diocletian from a drain 3ft below Westbury and a bronze coin of Constantine II from a garden behind Skippers public house at Terrace View, Horsecastles. A Roman bronze razor handle was discovered in 1931, 3ft 6ins below South Street, when Sherborne Gas Company dug a trench opposite the former Council Offices.

Midway between the Roman buildings of Lenthay and Pinford stands Sherborne Abbey (ST 638 165). As with many Anglo-Saxon buildings, notably at Exeter Cathedral to the west, Winchester Cathedral to the east, Bath Abbey to the north and Wimborne Minister to the south, there is every reason to think that the builders reused a Roman platform and materials. R.H. Carpenter told a meeting of the Royal Institute of British Architects in 1877 that he believed there was a Roman floor beneath Sherborne Abbey with the 'foundations of more than one building resting upon it.'

Coldharbour (ST 645 174), as a place name, commonly occurs beside Roman roads. Its location at Sherborne, beside a straight stretch of highway, is consistent with one of these unheated shelters or huts that were provided from post-Roman times as wayside refuges for travellers. Cold Kitchen, as on the Wiltshire downlands beyond Mere, is a variation of the term.

Immediately beyond Castleton parish, a substantial Roman building stood near East Farm (ST 593 152) on the north side of the road into Bradford Abbas. Professor James Buckman published his excavation report in 1878 and Charles Bean revisited the site with a spade in 1958. Buckman found heaps of broken stone tiles, quern stones and what he described as 'cooking stoves', plus a 'quantity of scattered tesserae'. He had not, however, come across the walls of the main buildings in what was then a 50-acre field. Bean struck lucky, finding herring-bone foundations and the remains of dressed stone walls, 2ft 2ins thick, that revealed a building 82ft long and 24ft wide. There was a flue in the south-east corner and Keinton blue marble flagstones paved the better preserved north-west corner. Finds included bronze and Kimmeridge shale bracelets and a bronze brooch with a spiral spring. As seems to be the case almost everywhere Bean went, his sharp eyes also alighted on a Bronze-Age barbed and tanged flint arrowhead, to go with stone axes already found on the site.

Ruins of this and adjoining buildings may well have been used as a boundary marker when parish lines were drawn in Anglo-Saxon times. The same applied to the even more extensive remains on the other side of the River Yeo, a mile south in flat lands midway between Thornford and Bradford Abbas. The Thornford Villa (ST 594 137) is just inside that parish from the point where it and the adjacent parishes of Castleton, Bradford Abbas and Clifton Maybank meet beside the river. The site was discovered and dug by Professor Sidney Savory Buckman in 1876 and has been under the plough ever since. Bean confirmed its position, for the benefit of the Ordnance Survey *Map of Roman Britain*, by exposing a tessellated pavement at a depth of 10 inches.

Finds from the villa, including stones reused for a medieval mill half a mile upstream, have been of the finest quality. The most remarkable, as a southern-British example carved in Ham stone, is a 25-inch frieze of three cloaked and hooded figures – the magi or wise men – which have their closest counterpart at Hadrian's Wall. The best preserved is bearded and is carrying a circular object that might be a severed head; the opposite end is badly abraded where it projected from the river bank.

# Three

## Seventh Century

Cenwealh, the King of the West Saxons who died in 672, was credited by John Hutchins, Dorset's eighteenth-century historian, with being one of the founders of a major church at Sherborne. The opportunity to do so became possible after 658 when the *Anglo-Saxon Chronicle* tells us he 'fought against the Britons at Peonnan, and put them to flight as far as the Parrett.' Peonnan appears to have been in a ridge of hills, perhaps at Penselwood, although King Arthur's legendary Camelot at Cadbury Castle also fits the topography.

The King and his coterie had been recently converted to Christianity by Saint Birinus. A Frank from Gaul, sent to Britain by Pope Honorius, he began his mission to Wessex in 634 and stayed until his death in 650. He was based at Dorchester-on-Thames which remained the seat of episcopal power until Cenwealh divided the growing diocese, in 660, by establishing Bishop Wini at Winchester in the Wessex heartlands. Winton remains the bishop's official name.

Agilbert, who followed Birinus into the post as bishop at Dorchester-on-Thames, was dismayed at the dramatic reduction of his powers and returned across the Channel 'to receive the bishopric of the Parisians, beside the Seine in Gaul.' As a result, the Dorchester see was abolished, and Winchester became the centralised power-base of the West Saxons.

King Ine succeeded to the kingdom in 688 and held it for 37 years. He was 'the son of Cenred, the son of Ceolwold, the son of Cuthwine, the son of Ceawlin, the son of Cynric, the son of Cerdic.' The King was also credited with establishing 'the Minster at Glastonbury'. For documentary and archaeological evidence at Sherborne we have to turn to the next century.

Logically, however, cathedrals are not bestowed on virtual green-field sites in the middle of nowhere. There must have been something sufficient, more than a tiny settlement, to have prompted and justified selection of a site for a church for significant promotion at the turn of the eighth century.

As with Winchester, the capital of the West Saxons, the almost non-strategic location of Sherborne was of considerable importance. Marauding Danes, liable to carry out raids from Rochester to Exeter and even up the Severn Sea, as it was known, made the coast too dangerous to contemplate. It may have been a further consideration that no easy landing-place had an obvious road heading straight for Sherborne. On the positive side, on the ground, there were a couple of important resources – water for mills and stone for building.

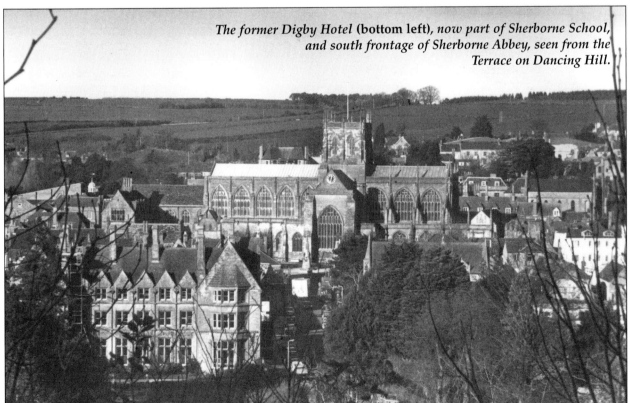

*The former Digby Hotel* (**bottom left**), *now part of Sherborne School, and south frontage of Sherborne Abbey, seen from the Terrace on Dancing Hill.*

# Sherborne's Countryside

**Background image:** *Ancient oak in woodland between the Camp and Jerusalem with members of the Crabb family, from Coldharbour, top and bottom.*

**Left:** *Meadows between Sherborne town and Sherborne Park, beside New Road, downstream from Castleton.*

*Blocked window of the medieval Chapel of St Emerenciana incorporated into Nethercombe Farm.*

*Black Labrador responding reluctantly to recall from the shallow waters of the River Yeo below New Road.*

**Centre right:** *West Mill, below Limekiln Farm, derelict in 1962.*

**Above:** *Boys from Sherborne School clearing debris at West Mill during its restoration in 1977.*

Right: *Geese at Pinford Farm waiting for Christmas.*

Below: *Present-day junction on Dancing Hill, looking north-westwards, with the shadowy line of the former course of the old road in the distance* (centre).

Below right: *Grain silos at Castle Farm, Castleton.*

Left: *Estate cottages beside Underdown Lane, on the ridge north from Dodge Cross, seen from Blackmarsh Farm.*

Below: *Sheep fold at Pinford Farm between Castleton and Goathill.*

Below: *Silverlake Farm, beside Lenthay Common, westwards to the fertile fields of Wyke and Bradford Abbas.*

Left: *Leafy length of the River Yeo, north-westwards, upstream to a glimpse of Castleton (centre).*

Centre left: *Family fishing on the Yeo between Gas House Hill and Castleton.*

Below: *Tree-covered Jerusalem Hill rising above fields of grain east of Sherborne Park.*

Bottom main: *The A352, with a Dorchester-bound bus, looking south-westwards to Limekiln Farm from Dancing Hill.*

Bottom left: *Ecclesiastical door (left) and window (right) at Nethercombe Farm, south-eastwards from Coombe.*

# Four

# Eighth Century

The name Sherborne, *Scirburna* from early Anglo-Saxon times – Latinised as *claros fons* in ecclesiastical documents – means 'clear stream'. That was the Coombe Stream which rises in Overcombe, midway to Sandford Orcas, and joins the Dymor Stream as it flows through the deep-cut valley of Coombe where it crosses an ancient road from Sarum and Shaftesbury to Ilchester and Somerton. This spot was in Nethercombe, below Greenhill. The road came into Sherborne from Pinford Lane, along Newland and through the Green, before dropping down Greenhill through Back Lane.

The combined flow of the watercourse from Coombe and Dymor was forded by the main road. It is now in a concrete culvert, below the A30 between the Swan Inn and Kitt Hill, and along the western side of Kennel Barton where the Sherborne monks established a series of fish-ponds. Then came Abbey Mill, its site under the science block of Sherborne School, from which a sluice could be opened as necessary to flush the monastic drains. Having passed the western side of the churchyard and the eastern end of the Almshouse it then weaved through Westbury. From the corner of Cook's Lane it continued southwards to join the River Yeo – *Fons Limpidus* to the monks – below the former Digby Hotel, to the west of Sherborne Station. This heads for the Somerset Levels where it joins the River Parrett and flows into the Bristol Channel at Bridgwater.

That was the basic scene and setting for one of England's premier Anglo-Saxon towns. Sherborne Cathedral, named for the 'cathedra' which was the bishop's seat, was dedicated to Saints Peter and Paul. It was a church with 'familia' – a religious household of clergy and their assistants – who seem to have had their household beyond the western end of the church, on the site of the later Vicarage in Abbey Court.

The see of Sherborne, created by dividing the huge Winchester-based West-Saxon diocese, covered the whole of the South West peninsula from western Wiltshire to beyond the Tamar, including the whole of the counties of Devon, Dorset and Somerset. The politics of division, driven by the logistics of expansion, was approved if not instigated by Brihtwaeld, Archbishop of Canterbury. The opportunity to put it into effect came in 705 with the death of Haedde, Bishop of Winchester, at a time when the victorious Wessex army had pushed the western frontier well beyond comfortable travelling distance of the capital. That remained the situation until 998 when further reorganisation and different sub-divisions saw Sherborne Cathedral becoming the Benedictine Abbey Church of St Mary the Virgin.

Several Victorian historians refer to the 'secular canons' of early Sherborne but Joseph Fowler (1872–1958), who retired to Sherborne in 1934, traced this to Bishop Tanner (1674–1735) and could find no earlier authority.

Stone for the cathedral came from the great workings beside Redhole Lane and the town's Bristol Road quarry – before there was a town named Bristol – in the valley towards Coombe. These workings continued for centuries until the area became known as Old Quarr. Pre-Conquest work belonging to Sherborne Cathedral is visible in the archway in the west wall of the north aisle. Greater than this masonry is the memory of Sherborne's first saint. He was a monk, the Abbot of Malmesbury, Wiltshire, from 675, who was promoted to be Bishop Aldhelm (639–709) of Sherborne.

By that time, in 705, he was already England's leading intellectual. It was a period when learning had gone out of fashion across much of Europe. Aldhelm, a first-generation Christian, was the son of Kenten who was related to King Ine. Born about the time when Birinus was making his West-Saxon conversions, Aldhelm kept the light of faith flickering with acclaimed verses that spread through England, Ireland and northern Gaul. A century and a half later they enthralled King Alfred (849–900).

On religious matters he was an orthodox spokesman for the Christian mainstream from which the Celtic tradition from across the water in Wales was in schism:

*The priests of Dyfed on the other side of the Severn Sea, boasting of their peculiar and special cleanliness of living, exceedingly abominate our communion, so much so that they do not deign to celebrate the offices with us in church, nor to partake with us of food at table in social friendliness.*

Aldhelm's life as a novice, in his thirties, was under Abbot Hadrian at Canterbury, which though generally known as St Augustine's was actually dedicated to Saints Peter and Paul. The same dedication was chosen for Sherborne Cathedral. Aldhelm referred to Hadrian as 'the venerable preceptor of my rude infancy'. He became an accomplished lute player. After a couple of years he moved to Malmesbury in the time of Abbot Maildubh, from Ireland, who was 'a holy man of our race'.

Aldhelm was later credited with five miracles, starting with a stretched beam at Malmesbury, and the rest on his visit to Rome in about 700. They included an 'out of the mouth of a babe' story in which a nine-day-old boy proclaimed that contrary to current public scandal he had not been fathered by Pope Sergius. A camel injured when it slipped while carrying a marble altar-slab, which was broken, and the said cargo were both repaired. The stone returned with Aldhelm to Wessex, where King Ine had it built into the newly-founded St Mary's Church at Bruton. The final miracle was 'stopping the storm' on a coastal journey from Canterbury to Dover, in 705, where he met vessels bringing materials for Sherborne Cathedral from Gaul.

William of Malmesbury, the Norman chronicler, records in his *Gesta Pontificum* that Alfred praised Aldhelm's English verses in the lost *Manual of Alfred*. Bishop Aldhelm is also known to have written heavier pieces in a mixture of Greek and Latin. His *De Laude Virginitatis* was addressed to the Abbess of Barking and her nuns. Nothing lighter has survived though there are some Latin verses that celebrate the completion of Sherborne Cathedral. These lines used to be thought to refer to Rome rather than Aldhelm's principal Dorset church. He also created the Romanesque Church of Lady St Mary at Wareham which was one of Britain's most substantially intact Anglo-Saxon churches until it was pulled apart in the name of restoration in 1841. The much smaller St Martin's Church in Wareham fared better, as did St Lawrence's Church in Bradford-on-Avon, which is now claimed as the earliest complete church in the country.

Bishop Aldhelm was an arbiter in defusing the fall out from one of the great schisms of the early Church – the method of calculating the date of Easter – and it was through his intervention that the Welsh finally conformed to the prevailing method. He made regular journeys across his diocese and it was on one of these that he died. The demise of Bishop Aldhelm was the main news for the *Anglo-Saxon Chronicle* in 709:

*In this year Aldhelm, who was bishop west of Selwood, died. Early in Daniel's time the land of the West Saxons had been divided into two dioceses, whereas it had previously been one. Daniel held one and Aldhelm the other. Forthhere succeeded Aldhelm.*

The two dioceses were of Winchester and Sherborne. King Ine of Wessex reinforced the western flanks of his kingdom by building a substantial fortress at Taunton. In 731 the *Anglo-Saxon Chronicle* traced the descent of Aldhelm, 'son of Ocga, the son of Ida, the son of Eoppa'. Aldhelm's son, Ecgwold, is then linked through Leodwold, Cuthwine and Cutha to the famous Ceolwulf, King of the Northumbrians.

Aldhelm would be translated to a saint, within 150 years, and his festival day is that of his demise which was 25 May 709.

He was travelling through Doulting, near Shepton Mallet, where a spring at St Aldhelm's Well surges from the stony slope below the Parish Church. This is said to be on the site of a timber church where he was taken when he was dying. Ecclesiastical associations were set to continue and one of the great barns of the Glastonbury Abbey estates stands nearby. Tradition has it that Aldhelm appeared to Bishop Ecgwine in Worcester Cathedral and summoned him to Doulting to take charge of the funeral arrangements.

The processional progress of the body, away from Sherborne, was via six overnight halting-places which included the churches Aldhelm had founded at Frome and Bradford-on-Avon. The cortège then joined the Fosse Way, the direct route across the Cotswold Hills, as they headed towards his Abbey at Malmesbury. Commemorative crosses were erected at each of the spots where the bier had rested for the night and these 'biscepstane' were still in place when William of Malmesbury was writing, 400 years later. Malmesbury has done less well than Sherborne, having failed to preserve any Anglo-Saxon masonry, which had received a similar but even more thorough Norman makeover. The precise site of Aldhelm's shrine, in the ruined eastern end of St Michael's Church, is unknown.

King Alfred enjoyed Aldhelm's secular writings and chuckled over his puzzles, such as this brain-teaser which successfully spans the centuries:

*A faithful guide I watchful keep the house.*
*In gloomy night I walk the dusky shades.*
*Scarce lose the sight of eyes in darkest caves.*
*For hated foes, who waste the heaps of corn,*
*I silent plan the crafty means of death.*
*On hunting bound I search the wild things' dens.*
*Not I with dogs will hunt the flying crowds,*
*For barking dogs wage cruel wars on me.*
*To hatred race it is I owe my name.*

The riddle gives the name 'mouser' which is the animal that more generally answers to the name of cat.

*Anglo-Saxon royal bones in the north transept of Sherborne Abbey.*

# Five

## Ninth Century

The West Saxons under King Egbert defeated the army of Beornwulf, King of the Mercians, in 'a great slaughter' at Wroughton in 825. Egbert then sent his son, Ethelwulf, and Ealhstan, Bishop of Sherborne, with his ealdorman Wulfhead and 'a large force' to Kent. From here they drove King Bealdred northwards, across the Thames, into Essex. The East Angles, meanwhile, killed King Beornwulf of Mercia and the people of East Anglia 'appealed to King Egbert for peace and protection'.

Abbot's Hill at Halstock was granted to the Bishop of Sherborne by King Ethelwulf in 841, being among 15 cassates of land that covered some six square miles. Half of this was arable and the remainder pasture and woods. Halstock provided chroniclers with the legend of St Juthware (or Judware) who is featured on page 489 of the medieval *Sherborne Missal*. This illuminated manuscript shows her kneeling after a family dispute as her brother beheads her for 'the testimony of Jesus'.

In martyrdom, with her head in her arms, she is seen offering it before the altar. Her remains are said to have been taken to St Wulfsin's Church in Sherborne. Wulfsin was Wulfsige III, Bishop of Sherborne, from 992 to 1001. In Halstock, Juthware was commemorated by the Quiet Woman Inn until it was delicensed at the end of the second Christian millennium. The sign showed her as a headless woman. Abbot's Hill (ST 532 097) overlooks the village from the north, on the Somerset border, and is known locally as 'Judith'.

Another two cassates, at Stoke Abbott, were granted to Bishop Ealhstan in Sherborne by Ethelwulf in 844. Again they account for a place name, near Beaminster, that survives as that of a village and parish.

Bishop Ealhstan resumed the role of military chaplain in 845, to ealdormen Eanwulf and Osric, when the 'people of the Dorset fought against the Danish army at the mouth of the Parrett' near Bridgwater, Somerset.

Ethelbald and Ethelbert were brothers of King Alfred. The former ruled the West Saxons from 855. He seems to have fallen out with the Church by marrying his father's widow in 858, although all was forgiven when he was laid to rest at Sherborne in 860 by Bishop Ealhstan. Sexual taboos were far from the minds of his people, according to the chronicler Henry of Huntingdon, as all England mourned and came to realise the extent of their loss. For he had given them a commodity that became a cherished memory – a

period of peace – and the year 860 saw Sherborne receiving two mentions in the *Anglo-Saxon Chronicle*:

> *In this year King Ethelbald died, and his body is buried at Sherborne. And then his brother Ethelbert succeeded in the whole kingdom and held it in good harmony. And in his time a great naval force came inland and stormed Winchester; and Ealdorman Osric with the men of Hampshire and Ealdorman Ethelwulf with the men of Berkshire fought against that army, and they put the army to flight and had possession of the battlefield. And Ethelbert reigned five years, and his body is buried in Sherborne.*

This led Sherborne historian W.B. Wildman to make a huge leap of wishful thinking, assuming that Ethelbert took refuge and regrouped in Sherborne, which became the capital of Wessex and remained thus until 878. Unfortunately for the Dorset claim, the chronicled reference is to aid coming from Berkshire, and the obvious next base was also in that direction, at Dorchester-on-Thames, Oxfordshire.

Ethelbert was certainly there, though thinking of Sherborne at the time, on 26 December 864. Holding court at the royal residence in Dorchester-on-Thames, attended by his brothers Ethelred and Arthur, he granted liberties 'to the holy foundation at Scireburnan'. Bishop Ealhstan was present to hear that henceforth his clergy were exempted:

> *... immutably and eternally, from all royal and judicial services, including the arrest of thieves, and all the irksomeness of secular labour, with the exception of military service and the construction of bridges.*

Ethelwulf's youngest son, the fifth and favourite, Alfred (849–900), had been taken by the King on a pilgrimage to Rome in 855. It can be assumed that he frequently visited Sherborne Cathedral for family funerals or to pay his respects at his father's grave. King Ethelbert and 'his two brothers' – Ethelbert and Alfred – were at Sherborne for Good Friday in 865. They met 'the assembled brothers, bold old and young'. The priests were named as Burghelm, Heoteman, Raednoth, Ethelheah, Oswuulf and Wistan, with an assistant named Coelmund.

Bishop Asser, who took over at Sherborne in 892, credited Ethelbert with reigning 'peacefully, amicably and honourably, mourned with great sorrow by all when he died.' That was in 866. Eanwulf, ealdorman of the province of Somerset, died in 867 and was buried 'in the monastery which is called Glastonbury'. Across the county boundary, the *Anglo-Saxon Chronicle* tells us, Bishop Ealhstan died. He had 'held the bishopric of Sherborne for 50 years, and his body is buried in the cemetery there.'

The 'wise warrior', as he was described by Bishop Francis Godwin, was credited by William of Malmesbury with having 'augmented the revenues of his bishopric wonderfully'. His successor, Heahmund, was a monk who had acted as chaplain to the royal court in Winchester and its northern residence at Dorchester-on-Thames. After Ethelbert's death, the kingdom had passed to his brother Ethelred, whose younger brother Arthur became a loyal deputy. Together they took the West Saxon army to Nottingham in 868 to help King Burgred and his beleaguered Mercians persuade their common enemy, the Danes, to return to York.

Bishop Heahmund also travelled with the army and was killed in battle. Together with 'many important men' he fell in 871. The West Saxon army, under King Ethelred and his brother Alfred, had fought the Danes at Ashdown, Basing and Merton. Heahmund was killed in the last engagement, after which 'a great summer army' met at Reading. Ethelred died 'after Easter' (15 April 871) and was buried in Wimborne Minster. King Alfred attended his brother's funeral in Dorset. One of the seven manuscript versions of the *Anglo-Saxon Chronicle*, that produced at Abingdon in the mid-eleventh century, gives Sherborne instead of Wimborne as the King's resting-place.

These were Alfred's wilderness years, in the swamplands of the pre-drained Somerset Levels, where combinations of tidal surges and flash-floods could inundate the landscape as far inland as Glastonbury and Wells. The western refuge of the West Saxons, pushed towards the Severn Sea by the inroads of the Danes, was along islands of higher ground strung like stepping-stones in marshland beyond the River Parrett. Their main camp, which is still linked to the next low ridge at Lyng by a causeway, was on a rounded hill at Athelney.

Aethelheah, who succeeded Heahmund at Sherborne, is most likely to have been the bishop who baptised the 30 Danes and their leader, Guthrum, after their resounding defeat at the Battle of Edington in 877. The act of capitulation and contrition took place at Aller, where the church stands on a hillock, towards Langport. They went to Wedmore and signed a treaty. Diplomacy came out of carnage as Guthrum was embraced by Alfred and proclaimed as his godson.

Wulfsige, the first of that name, followed Aethelheah at Sherborne. He was 'held high in esteem by Alfred' according to John Leland, centuries later, but that would have been a requirement for appointment. His successor, Bishop Asser, was that and much more. A Welshman, who entered monastic life at St David's, Pembrokeshire, he had been in Alfred's household from 885. There, in 893, he had written his *Life of Alfred*, and he became Bishop of Sherborne after the death of Bishop Wulfsige at the end of the century.

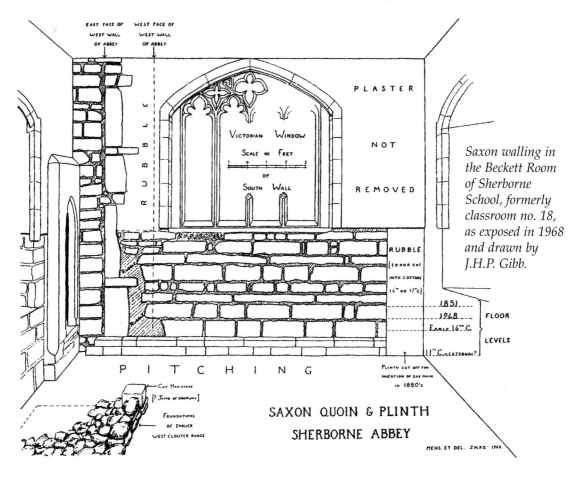

*Saxon walling in the Beckett Room of Sherborne School, formerly classroom no. 18, as exposed in 1968 and drawn by J.H.P. Gibb.*

**SAXON QUOIN & PLINTH SHERBORNE ABBEY**

# Six

## Tenth Century

The year 909 saw changes in both Wessex dioceses. The *Anglo-Saxon Chronicle* records that 'Frithustan succeeded to the bishopric in Winchester, and after that Asser, who was bishop of Sherborne, died.' With it came a big reform of the boundaries of the huge see of Sherborne to reflect the growing number of regional power centres that were emerging elsewhere in Wessex. The Sherborne diocese shrank to just the county of Dorset with new episcopal authorities being created at Crediton (Devon and Cornwall), Ramsbury (Wiltshire and Berkshire) and Wells (Somerset).

On the ground near Wyke, west of Sherborne, a length of dry ditch has remained a boundary for more than a millennium and marks the meeting point of the Digby and Winchester College estates. Its course, Joseph Fowler pointed out, corresponds with a dyke mentioned in a charter granted by King Athelstan – the first monarch of all England – on 26 January 933. He gave ten cassates of land, mainly around Bradford Abbas, including Aettandene (Aetta's Dean) and adjoining Loscombe, the dry valley south of it, to the Bishop of Sherborne.

The antiquary Thomas Hearne (1678–1735) found contemporary abstracts of these charters and other documents in the tenth-century *Sherborne Cartulary*. Its compilers, the clerks who went with Athelstan on his tours, were the founding members of the English civil service.

Sherborne's next entry in the *Anglo-Saxon Chronicle* was in 978: 'In that year Aelfwold, who was bishop of Dorset, died, and his body is buried in the Minster at Sherborne.' Remains of this structure were discovered by the architect R.H. Carpenter in the 1870s. Abutting the centre section of the Abbey's existing west wall are the footings of a substantial Anglo-Saxon tower, comprising a stone platform 33 feet long and 24 feet wide. Its south-west corner was rediscovered in 1949 by Sir Alfred Clapham (1883–1950) during the course of one of his last investigations on behalf of the Royal Commission on Historical Monuments.

King Edgar, and after him Ethelred II, both encouraged the Benedictines to expand their presence in England. In 998, Bishop Wulfsige III of Sherborne was persuaded to eject his secular clergy and to adopt the discipline of the Benedictine order. The wealthiest and most academic of religious communities, this was founded by Saint Benedict (480–547) in 529, when he established Monte Casino in Campania as the first of his 12 monasteries.

Rome-educated, from the Umbrian Apennines, he turned to asceticism at the age of 20. His *Regula Monachorum*, with rules of obedience and liturgy that he called the 'Opus Dei', formed the basis of western monasticism. 'The monk's life ought to be a perpetual Lent,' he decreed. Saint Augustine introduced the order to Britain in 596.

The imperative behind the change of status for Sherborne in 998, from cathedral to abbey, was the up-coming millennium and expectations that a religious kingdom might dawn. In celebration the relics of St Juthware – of the story from Halstock in Ethelwulf's time – were brought to Sherborne Abbey.

*Detail of the north wall of All Hallows Church and a shaft repaired with inset tiles.*

# *Wyke*

Right: *Sixteenth-century tithe and farm barns at Wyke, joined as a single building 230 feet long with 39 bays under a stone-tile roof, comprise the largest surviving relic of the former Abbey farms.*

Left: *Wyke House, built in 1650 by Eliab Harvey, stands on an earlier platform inside a medieval moat.*

Below: *Pastoral approach to Wyke Farm along the bridleway from Thornford.*

# Seven

# *Eleventh Century*

The *Sherborne Pontifical*, a Benedictine manuscript dating back from the founding of Sherborne Abbey, survived the Reformation and is preserved in the Bibliotheque Nationale, Paris. This 'Bishop's Book' contains a copy of a letter from Aethelric, Bishop of Sherborne from 1001 to 1012, explaining that the bishopric's historic endowment of 300 hides – in the region of 36,000 acres – had been reduced through the improvidence of his predecessors. Some ten per cent of the holdings, around Holcombe Rogus in Devon, had been 'alienated' with the result that the diocese could no longer meet its obligation to the kingdom, to provide and provision a longship for national defence.

Aethelric's letter may well overstate the losses and their implications as it was drafted for the purpose of soliciting a subsidy from Earl Aethelmaer. On the other hand, it is known that the transaction involving Holcombe Rogus, at the instigation of Bishop Aelfweald II of Sherborne, had been confirmed by Earl Godwine at a shire gathering in Exeter. The conveyance was to two Norsemen. They were Care, the son of Toki, and his brother and heir, named as Ulf. The transfer was a lease rather than a sale, as the land, produce and its workers were due to revert to the bishopric after two generations.

The requirement for providing a longship to fight with the fleet is explained by an extract from the *Anglo-Saxon Chronicle* in 1007: 'In this year the King ordered that ships should be built unremittingly over all England, namely a warship from 310 hides, and a helmet and corselet from eight hides.' By the end of the Anglo-Saxon era there were four tithings in Sherborne – Abbot's Fee, Westbury, Hound Street and Eastbury.

Hereman became Bishop of Wiltshire after the death of Bishop Brihtwold in 1045. Previously the Bishop of Ramsbury, Bishop Hereman then became Bishop of Sherborne after the death of Aelfweald, a monk from Winchester, in 1058. Hereman then sought to merge the sees of Dorset and Berkshire.

Over the winter of 1049–50, arriving in time for Easter, Bishop Hereman and Bishop Aldred went to Rome. They were on a mission for King Edward the Confessor. Explaining the situation in England, they pleaded with Pope Leo IX to release King Edward from a pledge to go on his pilgrimage to Rome.

Flemish by birth, Hereman proved to be a great survivor, and soon came to terms with his new Norman masters. Having taken part in the consecration of Edward the Confessor's new Westminster Abbey, on 28 December 1065, he returned there for the coronation of William the Conqueror on 28 December 1066.

Bishop Hereman tired of dividing his life between Sherborne and Ramsbury as he travelled around his sprawling double-diocese. He pointed out the benefits of having a new base midway between these geographical extremities. His chosen alternative was beside the River Avon in Wiltshire, where Roman roads converged on an Iron-Age hill-fort, which was being turned into a Norman fortress.

Amalgamation took place in 1075, after which both Sherborne and Ramsbury ceased to have bishoprics, and Sarum was paramount as it remains to this day, through the Salisbury diocese, though the original Sarum Cathedral is in ruins. The period of transition went on until its foundation, by Bishop Osmund, in 1091. Completion and dedication to Our Lady took place on 5 April 1092. It was replaced in the meadows by New Sarum which is Salisbury Cathedral. Episcopus Saresburiensis – Bishop of Sarum as it became through later contractions – retained the secondary office of Abbot of Sherborne. The tithes from Sherborne 'except the tithes and right of burial belonging to the monks' went to the new foundation.

The drought year of 1077 saw a hot summer in which 'wildfire came upon many shires and burned down many villages, and also many towns were burned down' – including London, early in August. That winter Bishop Hereman died, on 20 February 1078, and was buried at Old Sarum.

The estate held by the Bishop of Sherborne was listed and valued for fiscal purposes in the Domesday Book of 1086. As well as Sherborne (worth £50), the ecclesiastical lands included the adjoining manors of Oborne (£4), Over Compton (£6), Bradford Abbas (£10), Thornford (£5), plus Stalbridge (£12) and Stalbridge Weston (£7), Corscombe (£7) and Stoke Abbas (£6). These eight manors were to provide for the 'sustenance of the Sherborne monks'. In total, 43 hides had 46 plough teams, and the manpower included 53 slaves. The next up the scale were serfs, followed by cottagers, bordars and villeins. The latter, in Sherborne as in Cerne Abbas (see *The Book of Cerne Abbas*), had their houses beside Acreman Street which in both cases runs from north to south on the west side of the monastic complex. Acreman, as used by Aelfric in AD1000, equates to 'agricola' or farmer.

A hide, which had been originally defined as the ground needed to support one family, was given a physical definition in Domesday as a carucate of arable land (120 acres) plus its appurtenances of meadow, pasture, wood and waste. The Bishop of Sherborne's estate therefore amounted to upwards of 5,000 acres of cultivated land which was farmed in strips in the open-field system. As for the detail, the Conqueror's Commissioners show their independence and thoroughness by noting that three virgates (90 acres) with one plough, at Stalbridge, had been misappropriated by an exceedingly important person. The ground had been seized by the King's son and heir, William Rufus, without consent from either the bishop or the monks. Not the best loved of future monarchs he eventually met his arrow in the New Forest.

The sequel to the Norman Conquest was the creation of 'knight's fee' holdings in a measure to create a mounted yeomanry available for mobilisation and military service. The Sherborne knights included a Flemish batch which reflected the roots of Bishop Hereman: Edward (Anglo-Saxon), Grip (Danish), Inglebert (Flemish), Lambert (Flemish), Norman (Danish), Otbold (Anglo-Saxon), Randulf (Danish), Sinod (Anglo-Saxon) and Waleran (Flemish).

Norman rule was reinforced by a national gathering. Having knighted his younger son, Henry, in Westminster Abbey, King William travelled to Old Sarum for Lammas Day, 1 August 1086. Bishop Hereman provided his accommodation. Accompanied by privy councillors, King William met 'all the people occupying land who were of any account all over England.' One of the surviving versions of the *Anglo-Saxon Chronicle* goes into more detail and lists the elite as 'archbishops, bishops, abbots, earls, barons, sheriffs' who were escorted by their knights. Thousands attended what may have been the biggest gathering in the vicinity of Stonehenge to have taken place since the Bronze Age.

The first purpose of the 'Mickle Gemot', for William, was to have public swearing of 'oaths of allegiance to him, that they would be loyal to him against all other men.' The second reason, even more important, was that the Domesday Book was being put to its first test, to raise through taxation 'a very great amount of money'. This was to fund the King's departure – via the Isle of Wight – to his homeland and at the same time to raise an army to protect England from invasion and usurpers whilst he was gone. There were also natural calamities to contend with:

*And in the course of the same year, it was a very severe year, and a very laborious and sorrowful year in England; in cattle plague; and corn and crops were checked, and there was such great misfortune with the weather as cannot easily be conceived – there were such big thunderstorms and such lightning that many people were killed and it kept getting worse and worse among the people. May God Almighty make things better when it is his will.*

Storms, fever and pestilence persisted into the following year. These were seen as an omen which came to pass as William returned to Normandy shortly before the Feast of the Assumption of St Mary (15 August 1087). Within days he was desperately ill and his death took place 'on the day after the Nativity of St Mary' (9 September 1087). He was buried in the monastery he had built, St Stephen's, at Caen.

During the second half of the eleventh century, young Stephen Harding (1048–1134) was an oblate at Sherborne. The Anglo-Saxon youth had an unhappy time during his religious training at the hands of the Benedictine monks of the Abbey of St Mary. He fled to Scotland and from there to France. William of Malmesbury described him as 'more like a man fleeing from something that he dreads, than one who sought the thing he loved.'

Harding found his calling in Paris and with another student walked to Rome to prove the point in 1075. He found his destiny after befriending St Bernard and with St Robert de Molesmes co-founded the monastery of Clairvaux to the south of Dijon, France, in 1098. In 1110 Harding became its abbot.

A decade later he rewrote the rules, rejecting the hierarchical structure agreed at Cluny, and made a declaration of independence. His alternative *Carta Caritatis* – Charter of Love – rejected episcopal oversight and put the control of each religious house under the authority of its own abbot. By this declaration, returning to the basis of western monasticism as set by St Benedict, Abbot Harding had founded the Cistercian Order.

St Stephen Harding died in 1134. Back in his home country, Bishop Osmund died in 1099, and William II, nicknamed Rufus for his red hair, took up his legal rights during the ensuing vacancy of receiving Sarum's diocesan revenues. Similar accountancy interregnums took place at Winchester and Hereford as the King pondered or ignored the appointment of successors. There were none in the King's lifetime.

This was cut short by an arrow – commemorated at Rufus Stone in the New Forest – where William had been hunting deer. His companions fled and there was every reason to believe in conspiratorial assassination rather than careless accident.

*Details from John Siferwas' illustrations in the* Sherborne Missal.

# Eight

❖

# Twelfth Century

The result of the removal of William Rufus, for England and Sherborne, was the accession of Henry I and the rise of Roger de Caen. This was no ordinary churchman. He was talent-spotted by Henry I who was riding through Caen when he heard Mass being conducted at high speed. This, the King declared, made Roger the perfect man 'for a soldier's chaplain'. Then, as the Abbot of Sherborne, until 1112, he progressed through every major office in the corridors of power. These included Lord Chief Justice, Justiciar (Lord Treasurer), Lord Chancellor, and Regent of the Kingdom – '*secundus a rege*' – when the monarch was across the Channel in his role of Duke of Normandy.

Henry also appointed Roger as Bishop of Sarum, in 1102, although his consecration was blocked by resistance from the archbishops, and did not take place until 11 August 1107. 'Roger of Salisbury' stayed in post until his death in 1139 by which time he was generally known as 'Roger the Great'. He lived openly with his concubine, Matilda de Ramsbury, and their son Roger Pauper.

The Old Castle (ST 648 168), which gives its name to the parish of Castleton, was Roger's creation, but despite its importance he put Dorset firmly under the power of the Wiltshire-based diocese. This, the first Sherborne Castle, stands 'well couched' in strategic isolation on a 'rocky hillet' of flat-topped limestone between double streams and wide meadows.

Roger may well have come west to escape the militarisation of Old Sarum. His bolt-hole, built on the 'grand scale' that characterised everything he did, was to be a siege-proof home of his own on the closest suitable hill to the quaint and almost rustic household of previous Sherborne bishops. On its south side, on the slope towards Dinney Bridge and the Bradley Head mainstream of the River Yeo, he planted a vineyard which by 1146 was sufficiently productive to be subject to tithes.

Inside the castle, Bishop Roger had a private chapel, which was dedicated to St Michael, the commander of Heaven's army of angels and the candidate of choice for hilltop locations. Parts of its walls, inset with the chevron-moulding of a perfectly preserved Norman window, still stand. Castleton's first Norman Parish Church was built to the northeast, '*juxta castellum*' – outside the curtain wall – on a semi-detached knoll. This was dedicated to St Mary Magdalene and overlooks the three-acre meadow of Maudlin Close. A papal bull of Eugenius III refers to a second chapel dedicated to St Probus which seems to have been a chapel-of-ease in Castleton hamlet which soon acquired borough status.

Relations between the canons at Sherborne and those at the headquarters of the bishopric seethed for much of the century through disputes, jealousy and resentment which were displayed in equal measure on both sides of complex arguments. In 1122 an exceedingly busy Bishop Roger delegated his secondary office as Abbot of Sherborne to Thurstan to act independently in the future.

Roger also upset the Sherborne monks by building 'stew ponds' for fish and eels along the River Yeo between Castleton and Sherborne town. These disrupted the leats for two of the Abbey's three mills which ceased to turn. As compensation, the bishop granted them St Andrew's Mill, beside St Andrew's Church in Eastbury tithing, at the southern end of South Street. This stood on the west bank of the bishop's fish-ponds, just north of the present level crossing, on the site of Sainsbury's supermarket.

Nicholas, the sacristan at Sherborne Abbey, was granted the right to hold a five-day fair on either side of St Swithun's Day which was 15 July in the old-style calendar. St Swithun's Fair continued to benefit Nicholas' successors as vicar of Sherborne, until it was discontinued after Queen Victoria's golden jubilee, and Canon Lyon no longer received his £5 payment from Digby Estate Office.

Bishop Roger also created Lodbourne, cutting into the Abbey precinct along its south side, and provided exchange land 'two-fold' to the west in order to compensate for loss of space in the churchyard. Lodbourne, 'the street before the monastery of St Mary', is now Half Moon Street.

Sherborne Abbey, in the twelfth century, extended westwards from the west wall of the present building. Excavations between 1964 and 1967, on the site of what later became the medieval All Hallows Church, revealed its Norman twin towers. Dating from 1130, they lay to the north and south of the platform of the original Anglo-Saxon tower. The plinth for the northern tower emerged from beneath the wall of Abbey Close and also protruded into the fifth-form green of Sherborne School, where the exposed foundations of the north-west corner were seen by Dr Ralegh Radford on 20 July 1967. He made the pronouncement that the remains were definitely those of one of Bishop Roger's towers. Dr Radford paid his chance visit to Sherborne on the very afternoon when the three-year excavations were due to have been filled in.

Bishop Roger's early medieval fortress at Sherborne was similarly dominated by towers. Most of the stone came from the quarries on Ham Hill. It was completed in 1137 and John Leland, visiting four centuries later, was suitably impressed. He described it as moated, with drawbridges, and curtain walls in the shape of an octagon having:

*... four great towers in the castle wall, whereof one is the gatehouse. Every of them hath three lodgings in height. The great lodging is in the middle of the Castle Court, very strong, and full of vaults. There be few pieces of work in England of the antiquity of this that standeth so whole, and so well couched. One Bishop Langton made of late time, a new piece of work and lodgings of stone at the west end of the Hall; other memorable work was none set up since the first building.*

Bishop Roger also founded Devizes Castle (described as the most splendid in Europe), and rebuilt the castle surrounding his cathedral at Old Sarum. He then began a fourth fortress at Malmesbury. He added a great wall to the defences of the combined castle-cathedral complex inside the ancient earthworks at Old Sarum. King Stephen envied them and said he would give Roger half of England in exchange for his palaces, if asked, and that 'he will be tired of asking before I am of giving.'

This was after Henry's death, in 1135, as the country slid into an almost gentrified civil war between Stephen and his defiant barons, among whom Bishop Roger was one. Though he was retained as Stephen's Justiciar there were long-standing doubts about his loyalty in the event of Empress Matilda appearing in person to assert her right to the throne. This had been validated a decade earlier by Roger himself.

During 'the Anarchy', in 1139, Stephen seized Sherborne Castle and Bishop Roger's other fortress at Devizes. His other fortresses at Marlborough and Old Sarum also fell. Future Kings were no longer prepared to see Sherborne Castle held by a churchman and they upset a number of future bishops who asked for it back. It remained in royal hands until the time of Edward III. The events of 1139 destroyed Roger financially and physically. His son, Roger Pauper, was imprisoned and then exiled.

Bishop Roger died later that year, distressed and disgraced, and was succeeded by Jocelin de Bohun as Bishop of Sarum, whose lack of diplomacy and sensitivity exacerbated the rift between the canons of Salisbury and the monks in Sherborne. The matter went all the way to Rome, being presented in person by Abbot Robert from Sherborne, to a newly elected Pontiff Eugenius II in 1145. Knowing only one side of the argument he 'could express no opinion upon so doubtful a matter' but noted that if the tithes from Sherborne had been wrongly misappropriated for the benefit of Sarum, they should be 'restored to the monastery'. His Holiness delegated resolution of the issue to an independent inquiry conducted by Theobald, Archbishop of Canterbury, and Bishop Robert of Hereford.

There is no record of the adjudication but the monks had made powerful connections. Sherborne held the moral and spiritual high ground. Pope Eugenius II, as historian Joseph Fowler pointed out, was a Cistercian. He would therefore have realised that the founder of his order, St Stephen Harding, had started his vocation at Sherborne. By about 1150, Bishop Jocelin had backed down, and re-examined through written records and living memory the circumstances surrounding the investiture of Abbot Thurstan. Two witnesses from that time were called.

Brother Robert, Prior of Bremore, confirmed that Thurstan's 'allotted place, as a canon, in the choir at Sarum' was the key concern. His canons at Sherborne 'bore the Abbot's absenteeism badly'. They 'murmured against the Bishop in chapter, as much as they could and dared.'

The outcome by 1165 was the granting by Bishop Jocelin of two charters to Clement Thorncombe, Abbot of Sherborne. The latter was granted full right to the Prebend of Sherborne and apportioned land at Kingston. Monastic Kingstons include Abbot Street at Pamphill, behind medieval Kingston House, and Winterborne Kingston which still has its Abbot's Court Farm. The proviso was that payment of ten marks was reimbursed to Sarum each time a new abbot was appointed. This sounds like a typical British compromise. The charters also seek to clarify the function of the Abbot of Sherborne's 'vicarius' or priest-vicar, employed to perform his duties at Sarum Cathedral, specifying that he is to be of the 'habit and profession' of a secular canon. He lived in the 'house of residence' reserved for the Abbot of Sherborne in the precincts of the cathedral.

The Abbey's other out-stations ranged from a grange or working farm at nearby Wyke, where a long tithe barn survives, to a refractory cell for a prior and two monks – usually banished miscreants – at Kidwelly St Mary, near Swansea. Richard FitzWilliam, whose son Henry was a monk at Sherborne, gave three Welsh churches to the Abbot of Sherborne. These were at Kidwelly (All Saints), Penbray (St Elthut) and Penarth (St Ismeal). There was also a priory at Horton in Dorset. The former Abbey House there was given back to the Church in 1920, by the Earl of Shaftesbury, for use by Revd Richard Brome de Bary as his vicarage. The priors from Horton and Kidwelly travelled to Sherborne for special occasions such as the election of a new abbot.

On the south side of the town, Primsley Manor on Dancing Hill continued to function as a semi-autonymous unit, holding its own manorial court until 1654. This met twice a year 'at Michaelmas and Hocktide'. Primsley Manor Farm was renamed Dauncing Hill Farm in the sixteenth century, corrupted to Dancing Hill, and is still covered by a cluster of buildings, occupying a knoll bounded by a triangle of lanes, at what is now known as Limekiln Farm (ST 638 154). Between it and West Mill Lane, below the present raised causeway of the A352, the deep-cut line of its predecessor highway can be seen crossing the meadow to the west. It makes a graceful curve towards Limekiln Farm where it used to pass the buildings of Primsley Manor. 'Great Plumsley' survived as a field name and is shown on an 1834-dated estate map.

This was then a secondary road, to Thornford and Yetminster, as the earliest main route from Sherborne to Dorchester went southwards from South Street, up the Slopes and Gainsborough Hill. It survives as a stony public footpath and then a muddy bridleway, the wide double-hedged Green Lane, before being tarred as narrow Broke Lane between West Hall at Longburton and Folke across to the east.

The rights to the Primsley tithes were disputed in 1163 between Clement as Abbot of Sherborne and Jocelin de Bohun as Bishop of Sarum. These payments, with those of Haydon and Sherborne town, had for many years been collected by the abbot but Walter, as succentor of Sarum Cathedral and Prebendary of Axford in Wiltshire, produced evidence that they were rightfully his. Bishop Jocelin adjudicated at a hearing and delivered compromise arbitration in which the abbot could retain the tithes but would have to pay half a mark to the succentor at Easter and another half-mark at Michaelmas.

In order to avoid, or at least minimise, such disputes and to safeguard ownership of Church lands, a definitive property portfolio was kept in Rome. A papal bull, documenting ecclesiastical ownership, lists the Church of St Mary at Wimborne as being for the benefit of the Abbot of Sherborne. He also held St Andrew's Chapel at Wareham Castle and Holy Trinity Parish Church, beside Abbot's Quay, in what had been Dorset's major Anglo-Saxon walled town. As for Sherborne Castle, that is listed as a possession of the Bishop of Sarum with the claim continuing throughout the time it was confiscated by the monarch. Church and Crown resumed their uneasy alliance and Sherborne Castle became the designated residence of the Sheriff of Somerset and Dorset.

The twelfth century is the period from which we can start to put faces to names. Though only the head and a moulded arched top survive, in polished grey Purbeck marble, the representation of Abbot Clement in Sherborne Abbey is notable as being one of the earliest of monumental effigies. Clement Thorncombe was the brother of William Thorncombe who founded the chapel to St Thomas the Martyr on the Green. His effigy dates from about 1160 and shows thick curly hair and a beard. His head rests on an inscription with a Latin pun which loses a little of its impact in translation: 'May Clement find the Almighty clement to him; In whose lifetime this house was ruled with vigour.'

The *Sherborne Cartulary*, a tenth-century-through-to-the-twelfth-century collection of manuscripts from the Abbey, is preserved in the British Museum. It is from this, particularly for details on Bishop Roger and the 'good works' of William Thorncombe (Latinised as *Spyneuaus*), that much of our background information has come.

The abbot's fish-ponds, which receive many medieval mentions for eels and carp, provided the fish dish for the monks' Friday meal when meat was barred from the menu by Christian ordinance. The little lake – called the Cristall Well, in the anonymous Elizabethan poem 'Willobie his Avisa' – was on what John Leland called 'the River of Schirbourne' – between School House garden and the Yeatman Hospital. The once-clear waters of the stream from Coombe, which had given Sherborne its name, had become 'little better than a solution of mud' by 1866 and were blamed for a typhoid epidemic in Acreman Street the following year. This led to the stream being put into a culvert in 1873, with the exception of a swimming-bath for Sherborne School, where the 'pea-soup contents' were filtered once a fortnight.

In 1177 William Thorncombe, the son of Alfred Thorncombe, founded and funded the Chapel of St Thomas à Becket on the Green in Sherborne in honour of the Archbishop of Canterbury who was murdered in his own cathedral on 29 December 1170. Though Thorncombe was the sacristan of Sherborne Abbey, this was a titular rather than a ministerial post, linked to the fact that his brother, Clement Thorncombe, was Abbot of Sherborne. The contemporary Bishop of Sarum, Jocelin de Bohun, had taken Henry II's side in the bitter dispute between Becket and the King.

Whilst Becket was out of the country, Bishop Jocelin assisted the Archbishop of York, Roger of Pont L'Eveque, in crowning the King's eldest son, Prince Henry, in direct contravention of the practices and privileges of Canterbury Cathedral. Jocelin was among those excommunicated by Becket and had his sentence confirmed by Pope Alexander IIII who also relieved him of episcopal responsibilities.

Jocelin weathered the storm and came to Sherborne on 11 September 1177 to dedicate St Thomas the Martyr's Church. As part of his penance he also endowed the chapel with 45 acres of arable land. Three acres were on the Bishop's Home Farm and the remainder in strips split between the two open fields west and north-west of the town. One of the fields was under winter cultivation and the other reserved for spring sowing. Walter Proutfoot was the first rector of the new church, presented by the Bishop of Sarum, but after his death the advowson passed to the Abbot of Sherborne. Priestlands Lane and Priestlands, on the west side of the lower end of Bristol Road, preserve the memory of the rector's glebe lands.

Bishop Jocelin eventually retired in 1183 and spent the final year of his life in the Cistercian convent of Forde Abbey at Thorncombe where he died on 18 November 1184. Long after the politics had been forgotten the 'Canterbury Pilgrimage' remained the most popular in Christendom until this, with the rest of the nation's shrines, was destroyed by order of Thomas Cromwell, Vicar-General for Henry VIII, in 1538.

Joseph Fowler proved that the medieval Julian-on-the-Green, used as a public library in the twentieth century, was never a chapel – as had been supposed – nor was a garage behind nearby Georgian buildings. This also applied to a gazebo north of the stable block behind the Antelope Hotel. By producing a pencil drawing of 1802 by John Buckler of the New Inn (executed whilst the building was still intact), Fowler was able to prove that both of these incorporated carved masonry from the old New Inn.

On the other hand, he conceded that the chapel had been 'by the New Inn', as mentioned by John Leland on his visit to Sherborne in 1540. By this time, in the midst of the upheavals of Reformation, it was 'uncelebrated' (disused). John Hutchins noted that 'some remains' were still standing in 1750, 'where there is now a wheelwright's shop, between the Angel Inn and the top of Cheap Street.' The Angel Inn became a dormitory for Sherborne School and the

top of Cheap Street is the section beside the Newland junction. This places St Thomas the Martyr's Church in the vicinity of the bus stop in the middle of the south-west-facing part of the Green, in the triangle of thatched and other buildings between it and Greenhill to the north and Higher Cheap Street to the east.

Bishop Hubert Walter brought fresh thinking to the recurrent Sarum-Sherborne dispute in 1191. He discussed the matter with the abbot, William of Stoke, and established an inquiry. The outcome was an exchange of charters under which Sherborne conceded churches at Lyme and Halstock to finance a Prebend in the cathedral. In return, to mitigate the 'poverty and indigence' of the monks, the Abbot of Sherborne was to be given future control of the churches of Stalbridge and Stoke Abbas. This was conditional on the 'vicars-perpetual' of these parishes being provided with 'a reasonable stipend'. Bishop Hubert realised that in pacifying his troublesome monks he had to avoid creating a new under-class of impoverished clergy. There was also a pension fund for the monks. Payment of two marks annually was to be made from the church at Corscombe once it had fallen vacant. Amounting to £1.6s.8d., this sum was still being paid in 1539, when time was called for the religious houses.

*The surviving Anglo-Saxon walling of Sherborne Abbey is in the western end.*

# ✤

# Nine

# *Thirteenth Century*

Alan de Whittona, acting for Hubert de Burgh, was the under-sheriff at Sherborne Castle in 1200. In 1207, Ralph de Bray was in residence, on behalf of William Briwere who was Sheriff of Somerset and Dorset. Their supplies and arms held at Sherborne, in the custody of Eudo Martel acting as constable, were transferred to John the Marshall (1170–1235) following the signing by King John of the Great Charter in the Thames meadows at Runnymede on 15 July 1215. John received the castles at Sherborne and Dorchester in return for relinquishing those at Norwich and Oxford.

Appointed by John, Peter de Maulay was briefly in residence at Sherborne Castle as Sheriff of Dorset, but the King died on 19 October 1216. Peter de Maulay was forced to quit Sherborne by William Marshal, 1st Earl of Pembroke. Acting on behalf of boy-King Henry III, he awarded Sherborne Castle and the county of Somerset to William de Longespee, 3rd Earl of Salisbury. William Longsword, illegitimate son of Henry II and Rosamund Clifford – 'Fair Rosamund' – died at Old Sarum in 1226 and was given pride of place, with a recumbent effigy in chain armour, in partly-built Salisbury Cathedral. Henceforth the Bishop of Sarum was known as the Bishop of Salisbury though he retained 'Sarum' as his signature. Peter de Maulay went on to take up the crusader sword and sailed for the Holy Land where he died in 1241.

Adam of Barking, a Benedictine monk in Sherborne Abbey in about 1217, was praised by John Leland, Henry VIII's touring archivist, for his promise as a writer of both prose and verse. Leland draws attention to his scholarly side but others picked up on his moral zeal. The titles of many of his works are known but almost all of these manuscripts were subsequently lost. That includes the three works that Leland found in the library at Sherborne Abbey. These were the prose text *Super Quatuor Evangelia* and collections of verses entitled *De Natura Divina et Humana* and *De Serie Sex Aetatum*.

By 1223, Gilbert de Staplebridge was serving as the under-sheriff on behalf of the Bishop of Salisbury, Richard le Poore, who in his other capacity as Sheriff of Dorset then resumed ecclesiastical occupancy of Sherborne Castle. He had to put it in writing to the Crown that he was there by licence rather than right. The reason for a return to the western arm of the diocese was that the greatest ever changes were taking place in its midst. There he was organising the building of a replacement Salisbury Cathedral in the meadows at New Sarum. Richard le Poore was also a writer, addressing his *Ancren Riwle* – Rule for Anchoresses – to the reclusive nuns of Tarrant Abbey, at Tarrant Crawford.

Newland dates from this, being a borough created by Bishop Richard le Poore, in 1228. It was built from the Green at the top end of Cheap Street, south-eastwards across arable land, to Castleton. The logic of the location was to provide artisan accommodation and services to link the town and its castle. Newland was provided with its own chapel-of-ease, St Swithun's Church, 'at the cross' on the south side of the street between the present St Swithun's Road (ST 641 168) and a point opposite the Avenue. John Hutchins' editors, publishing the posthumous second edition of his county history in 1815, refer to 'a timber yard where human bones are found'.

Bodies are also said to have been uncovered when St Swithun's Road and North Road were built. The spot was again disturbed in 1955 for the building of a new house beside the junction of Newland and St Swithun's Road. At least 15 bodies were found in the foundation trenches, of all ages from children to the elderly, and the surrounding ground contained numerous sherds of fourteenth-century pottery. There was also a contemporary silver-gilt oval brooch set with garnets.

Near the church stood 'the cross' – later called 'the stone' – where borough court proceedings were held in the open air each May Day under the authority of the bishop's seneschal or steward. It stood at the east end of a triangle of open space, known as St Swithun's Fairground, midway between the Green and Castleton. Beside it were the triple apparatus of justice and punishment – the gallows, pillory and ducking-stool.

Here the burgesses were 'amerced and punished' and 'tallied and taxed' and were no longer accountable to 'the ancient vill' of Sherborne. Such 'Law Day' proceedings would continue until the Elizabethan times. Courts and fairs were also held at Castleton.

On 4 May 1240 King Henry III granted Bishop Robert Bingham and his successors the right to hold the fair of St Thomas the Martyr annually in Sherborne. It was a six-day fair, spanning both sides of the actual saint's day on 7 July, disregarding whether any of these was a Sunday. It was held on the Green and therefore became known as the Green Fair. The site of nearby St Thomas' Chapel became known as the Fair Field. This fair was one of those scheduled for abolition under the Fairs Act of 1871.

The historian Joseph Fowler wrote almost poetically on the growth of Cheap Street, as the town's main thoroughfare downwards and southwards from the Green 'on which Sherborne is strung like a bean on a string.' Its name, in Old English, was for the Market Street. The originally 'Cheeping' version of the word survives to this day at Chipping Norton and might have done so in Dorset, until Chipping Blandford was given a pretentious Latin tag and renamed Blandford Forum.

Repair and refurbishment at Sherborne Castle required huge quantities of timber as well as stone. Most of the wood came from Blackmore Forest where master carpenter Stephen de Estinton had the choice of the King's trees 'at Hartlegh' – named for 'the legend of the White Hart' which is also kept alive by the place name King's Stag – around Holnest and Middlemarsh. Whitfield, near Lillington, provided extra supplies for scaffolding, stairs and roofing when Estinton restored the Hall. By 1251 he had moved on to 'the Queen's Room, King's Houses and King's Chapel.' There were no longer any mentions of Bishop Roger, the original builder, and the new Roger was the chaplain, Roger de Cunnoc 'then ministering in the King's Chapel of St Michael within the castle.'

Barbicans and the four 'turellia ballii' forming the corner turrets of the outer defences were rebuilt 'on account of the immediate peril of the times' as Ralph Russel, the constable, was ordered to maintain an armed guard. On horseback he had on call ten mounted serjeants-at-arms, whilst for the watching brief from the battlements he had ten archers.

In 1261, Richard de Hasselburg from Haselbury Plucknett, Somerset, was seized and imprisoned in Sherborne Castle for 'making war against the King'. Having been convicted of felony, at Westminster, he was taken out into Sherborne Park and beheaded. His body was then suspended by the feet from the scaffold on Gallows Plot.

The Sheriff of Somerset, William Wake, had to leave the castle in 1267 when Edmund Couchback,

*Twelfth-century south-west gatehouse to the Old Castle, in the trees, as a romantic ruin in Victorian times.*

crusader son of Henry III, was given the new title of Governor of Sherborne Castle. The castle became a prison, holding Almaric de Montfort among others, with the constable, John de Somerset, being instructed to set aside the Outer Bailey for hutted accommodation in which the Sheriff of Dorset could hold 'the King's prisoners at the King's pleasure'. During the reign of Edward I these included Welsh hostages and prisoners of war from the Scottish campaign which had reached Falkirk and brought back as a trophy 'the Stone of Scone on which Scotch Kings are crowned.'

The Purbeck marble effigy of an abbot, in Mass vestments in the south choir aisle of Sherborne Abbey, dates from the mid-thirteenth century and is probably Laurence de Bradford, Abbot of Sherborne from 1246 to 1260. The figure is defaced and damaged with the exception of the finely-carved crosier.

Before 1279, the town's market-day was already established, on Thursday, and the Bishop of Salisbury held the right to stage four annual fairs. These were for two days at the Feast of the Relics; two days at St Swithun's Tide (granted by Henry I); six days at the Feast of the Translation of St Thomas the Martyr (granted by Henry III on 4 May 1240); and two days at the Feast of the Nativity of the Blessed Virgin Mary.

The century ended with disputes between the monks and the townspeople over joint use of the Abbey Church for monastic and parish purposes. As a result, until the Reformation, a physical barrier was erected at the west end of the present church and the Norman building further to the west became All Hallows Parish Church – although it had not been built, or was still unfinished, when Simon de Ghent, Bishop of Salisbury, passed through Sherborne en route to Chardstock in the far west of the county.

There was also a royal visit. Edward I was at Sherborne Castle on 28 March 1297, which turned into a working day with advisors and clerks, as letters were dispatched to Pope Boniface and the Bishop of Durham, among others.

# Sherborne Old Castle

Above: *Castle Court, at what is now the Old Castle, as a Bishop's Palace in the 1300s.*

Top right: *From Castle Court and its Hall Range to the south-west gatehouse* (centre).

Right: *The northern side of Castle Court, the best preserved part of the Old Castle, and its surrounding domestic buildings.*

Below: *Steps up through the original north gate and Barbican, flanked by walls four feet thick.*

Left: *Ruins in silhouette, westwards from the site of the south-east tower, to the south-west gatehouse (left), with the remainder comprising the Hall Range and Castle Court.*

Below: *Capital column and vaulted undercroft supporting domestic buildings in Castle Court.*

Bottom: *Remains of the north-east gate, south-eastwards across the dry moat, to the cedars of Sherborne Park.*

Right: *Massive foundations of the original entrance to the Old Castle, midway along the northern side, with a fortified staircase passing through a stout Barbican.*

Above: *Attendants and emblems of Sherborne, England, and Sherborn, Massachusetts (towards top left) as the focus of a scene in the 1905 Pageant held in the ruins of the Old Castle.*

Below: *Final tableau with the huge cast lining up behind shields at Sherborne Pageant in the Old Castle grounds.*

L.N.P. inventing it.

Left: *'L.N.P. inventing it' – the contemporary caption to this cigar-smoking caricature of schoolmaster Louis Napoleon Parker writing the Sherborne Pageant in 1905.*

**Right:** *Across the Bailey from the foundations of the north-west gate to Castle Court and the south-west gatehouse (left).*

**Left:** *Northwards from the footings of the Kitchen Range and remnants of Hall Range to the bigger walls of Castle Court.*

**Left:** *Westwards along the best surviving length of curtain wall to the south-west gatehouse.*

**Background image:** *The Old Castle as a parkland feature, glimpsed between weeping willows, from the corner of the Capability Brown grounds that grace the replacement Sherborne Castle.*

*Ruins in silhouette, westwards from the site of the south-east tower, to the south-west gatehouse (left), with the remainder comprising the Hall Range and Castle Court.*

✦

# Ten

# *Fourteenth Century*

Simon de Ghent, Bishop of Salisbury, was granted the right to hold an additional market in Sherborne, on a Tuesday, by King Edward I in 1300. The earliest reference to the new All Hallows Church, also by Simon de Ghent, appears in August 1303. He expressed concern at the growing number of unconsecrated parish churches in Dorset and mentioned those at Alton Pancras, Beaminster, Bere Regis, Fordington, Netherbury and Sherborne. Churches were not allowed to hold divine services if they had remained unconsecrated for more than two years. Newly-built All Hallows therefore dates from c.1301.

Its jagged remains project from the west wall of Sherborne Abbey and its reduced north wall forms the northern side of Abbey Close. The building was pulled down after the Dissolution of the Monasteries freed the Abbey itself for the use of the townspeople. The site of All Hallows, now under tarmac and turf, was put to use as a graveyard from 1555–1856.

The limits of 'la Newland', Sherborne's new town, included arable fields which extended to Hound Street. In the other direction, north-west of the Green on the ridge overlooking Coombe Stream, was the monks' Barton Farm. An *Inspeximus* was granted by Bishop Roger de Mortival, Bishop of Salisbury from 1313 to 1330, but this merely confirms Richard de Poore's original Newland charter. Burgesses held land in plots '20 perches in length and 4 perches in depth' with restrictions on their resale to 'churches, religious houses or Jews'.

Payment for tenancies was by fixed rent that was payable monthly. These were copyhold agreements, the title deriving from an entry copied from the relevant Court Roll. Such procedures resulted in place names such as Copyhold Lane at Winterbourne Abbas which have endured to the present day – though as a form of tenure it was consigned to the history books in the nineteenth century.

The earliest Newland document, written in Latin in 1305, reads in translation:

*To the court of Newland held on the Monday next after the Feast of the Translation of Blessed Thomas the Martyr in the 34th year of [King] Edward, John le Stut comes and surrenders into the lord's [lord of the manor] hand a certain holding in la Newland for the use of William Leghton and Juliana his wife. The same William and Juliana come to give to the lord for the right of entry two shillings, by pledge of Robert de Sydling and Richard le Reed.*

The Sheriff of Dorset was authorised on 1 April 1308 to spend 50 marks on urgent repairs to 'the walls of the King's Castle at Shireburn, and the houses and bridges of the same.' At that time, from 10 July 1307 until 18 January 1309, William, Archdeacon of Teviotdale, was held prisoner in the Sherborne Castle. He was then taken to the Tower of London where he died before Scottish fortunes turned at the Battle of Bannockburn. Reginald de Frome was held at Sherborne in 1326.

Abbot Hugh 'went the way of all flesh' on 23 April 1310 and was laid to rest in Sherborne Abbey. A remarkably detailed account of how his replacement was appointed was copied into diocesan records by Simon de Ghent. Two Sherborne monks, Geoffrey de London and John de Thornford, and their Precenter, travelled to London to obtain King Edward's licence for the brotherhood to elect a successor. In the meantime, Brother Richard de Mohun took charge of the house as Prior. He announced on 6 May that the following Wednesday, 13 May, would be the election day. The priors in the Abbey's cells at Kidwelly, Pembrokeshire, and Horton in Dorset were summoned to attend. On the Wednesday, by 'immemorial custom', Prior Richard presided over a solemn assembly in the Chapter House.

Seven *compromissarii* or deputies were authorised to decide the matter. They were Richard de Mohun (Prior of Sherborne), Richard de Chynnock (Sub-Prior), Geoffrey de London (Cellarer), John de Compton (Prior of Horton), Philip de Dunster (Brother), John de Wells (Brother), and Nicholas de Wells (Sub-Sacristan). They consulted with others who were present, including Philip de Bridport, Henry de Cerne, Robert de Domdaunt (Kidwelly monk), Philip Ellis (Horton monk), Thomas Louf, William de Milton, Robert de Orchet, Edward de Querendon (representing Richard de Cocker, Prior of Kidwelly), Robert de Ramsbury (Chamberlain and future Abbot of Sherborne), John Tresk, Henry de Wimborne and Robert de Woolmington. Age or infirmity prevented the attendance of Brother John de Reading and Horton monk John de Littleham. Brother William Osmund, in Kidwelly Priory, 'did not trouble to appear' though the distance from the west of Wales to Sherborne might seem to have been a reasonable excuse.

The seven monks who were to decide the matter huddled on stone benches as they deliberated the merits of those 'within the bosom of the monastery' – including themselves – until John de Compton declared that they were agreed. John de Thornford was duly elected. 'Fully 30-years-old, prudent, discreet, lettered, blameless in life and morals and wise alike in spiritual and secular affairs,' he was 'a professed monk of the Order of St Benedict'. He showed suitable demur and reluctance until persuaded to accept the office laid upon him 'for the honour of God and Blessed Mary our Lady Patron.' Singing *Te Deum*, the monks led him to the altar in the Abbey, where Master John de Tarrant, representing the Dean and Chapter of Salisbury, announced the result to applause from the clergy and laity.

Notification of John de Thornford's election was sent to the Bishop of Salisbury the following day with the request that it be confirmed with the seal of Episcopal benediction. John de Thornford appeared before his bishop, in a hospice chapel near St Bridget's Church on 20 May 1310. Bishop Simon seems to have been in hospital with failing health although he lived until 1315. He found a problem, however, as John de Thornford was not accompanied by a procurator from Sherborne who could vouch that a proper election had been held.

As a result the matter was postponed. The process resumed on Friday 12 June 1310 in Reading Abbey. Brother Orchet, from Sherborne, appeared with John de Thornford bearing a letter from the Prior and his fellow monks. The royal mandate was issued the following Monday. Formal acceptance of Bishop Simon's benediction took place at Reading on 21 June 1310, the Sunday after the Feast of the Holy Trinity, when John de Thornford proclaimed obedience and subjection to Bishop Simon and 'the Holy Church of Salisbury'.

As well as serving his bishop, the Abbot of Sherborne and Convent of St Mary also had obligations to the King, particularly in providing 'corrodies' or retirement homes for former royal retainers. Edward II sent Hugh Cade in 1315 to replace Richard le Potager who had died. Robert de Sandwich and Hugh de Windsor followed in 1315. When John de Compton was elected Abbot of Sherborne in 1330, one of his first arrivals to claim a pension was 'one of the King's clerks', namely Martin de Exning. Richard de Sauser, in 1335, was followed by John Teissant and then Adam de Sherborne, in 1338. William de Percy, a parson from Folke, had a chamber with hearth, chimney and latrine, plus access to the monks' laundry. He was succeeded by John de Bradford, a chaplain, in 1366.

Such accommodation, provided for life, came with daily provisions of a large quality loaf, 'pastus, and the best convent ale'. Inhabitants were dressed in robes of striped cloth with fur, replaced each St Andrew's Day, in the style of 'the suit of the esquires and clerks of the Abbot and Convent.'

From 14 July 1317, for the next four decades, the Abbot of Sherborne acquired a variety of parcels of lands and tenements for which the conditional licence fee was the founding of a chantry. Its chaplain was required to say Mass daily in Sherborne Abbey for the souls of the late Edward II and his household steward Robert Fitzpaine. Local properties acting as its endowment were at Leigh and Stalbridge but 'Bere' has to be Beer in Devon rather than Bere Regis in Dorset, given it comes with mentions of Seaton adjoining. From here, on the Jurassic coast, came hard fine-grained chalky stone that was easily carved and the ideal replacement for that from Caen in Normandy (the supply of which stopped after the Norman French balked at their invasion of England having been inverted by English colonialism). The chantry inside Sherborne Abbey was dedicated to St Nicholas.

Ownership of the Old Castle at Sherborne was transferred by the Crown in 1337, to William Montagu or Montacute, 3rd Baron Montacute and 1st Earl of Salisbury (1301–44). He had been its constable since 1330 when he received lands forfeited by Roger de Mortimer, 1st Earl of March. William Montagu had been a bodyguard of Edward III in countering the Scottish invasion of 1327, and then accompanied him to France, following which he entered Nottingham Castle via an underground passage and found Mortimer in the Queen Mother's apartments.

The Bishop of Sarum, Robert Wyville, disputed the King's right to have sold a building which, he maintained, had been wrongly seized from the Church. He sued William Montagu or Montacute, 2nd Earl of Salisbury (1328–97) in the King's Court for unlawful retention of the property in November 1354. Accusations of 'dishonour' almost led to combat, in the form of jousting for ownership of the building, but the bishop wisely avoided fighting. Young William, in 1350, became one of the original Knights of the Garter and took part in beating the Spaniards off Winchelsea. Wyville offered a compromise. By paying 2,500 marks to William to quit his claim, plus 500 marks to King Edward III – a total of £2,000 – he successfully restored religious ownership in 1355.

Edward, Prince of Wales (1320–76), the Black Prince, rode into Sherborne Castle on 15 May 1357. There, with Sherborne as its date line, the victor of Crecy and Poitiers – 'Le Neoir' to the French from the colour of his armour – wrote a letter on a more prosaic matter, concerning unrest in Chester. Having sailed from Bordeaux to Plymouth, he was accompanied by his prisoner, King John of France, en route to London which the Black Prince entered in triumph on 24 May 1357. Word of his famous battle-cry had travelled ahead of him: 'Banner, advance, in the name of God and St George!'

Bishop Wyville died on 4 September 1375 and his memorial is a 90-inch brass in the Morning Chapel at Salisbury Cathedral which features him in ecclesiastical splendour, seated in the middle of his fortress at

Sherborne. It had become his residence for visitations and travelling in and around Dorset.

The importance of Sherborne in national affairs is shown by the fact that three men from the town attended the Westminster Assembly for the Parliament of 26 September 1337. They were Adam de Lyveden, Richard atte Slade and William Turpyn.

The next account of Sherborne residents appearing in Westminster comes from 1383 when the burgesses of Newland challenged the feudal right of Ralph Ergham, Bishop of Salisbury, to impose autocratic and onerous restrictions on their emergent civil liberties. Before the King's Justices they disputed the imposition of tellage on beer production. This tax was known as 'crookpenny' from the Bishop's crosier.

Matters had come to a head when the Bishop's rent collector confiscated a horse in an act of distraint in lieu of arrears in crookpenny payments. No one then fed or watered the animal and it died three days' later. The burgesses lost their case and the Justices upheld the Bishop's 'rights and services'. Crookpenny continues to appear in the town's medieval records through to Elizabethan times, when Hugh Meyer was the rent collector, in 1568.

Cowleaze Gate, an acre of land below Harding's House Lane in Coombe Bottom, was given by Thomas Bylk to Robert de Bridport, an Exeter merchant, in 1350. The significance of this transaction is that the plot survives – as a hedged rectangle but originally a strip of open field – and marks the boundary of the medieval tithings Overcombe and Nethercombe in the fork between the two lanes.

Chapel Hill at Overcombe, facing its farmhouse, preserves the memory of St Peter's Chapel. The chapel at Nethercombe survives, on the east side of Coombe Road, and was dedicated to St Emorentia. Newell, below Nethercombe, takes its name from 'the New Well' and its waters flow below Hospital Lane and through a culvert under South Street. Here it passed the town's other medieval chapel, St Andrew's Church, beside the mill opposite the Woolmington Hotel, since renamed the Pageant.

The Julian on the Green, built as a hospice, was provided by Sir Stephen Derby who represented the county of Dorset in Parliaments from Edward III in 1369 to the third gathering in the time of Richard II, in 1394. He was present when the Commons elected their first Speaker, Peter de la Mare, in 1377.

From 1387 there is an inventory of 'Servants of the Convent' and 'Servants of the Abbey' listing some 30 employees of Sherborne Abbey and giving their wages at Hocktide (second Monday and Tuesday after Easter, significant in Sherborne as a day for celebrating victory over the Danes) and Michaelmas (Feast of St Michael, 11 October in the old calendar; now 29 September). The latter has been chosen here for purposes of comparison and the first ten entries are for employees of the convent with the remainder being ascribed to the Abbey:

| Cook: | 4s.0d. | Drover: | 2s.0d. |
|---|---|---|---|
| Infirmary servant: | 2s.0d. | Wood carriers: | 6s.0d. |
| Church servants: | 2s.0d. | Manure carrier: | 2s.0d. |
| Three carters: | 7s.6d. | Swineherd: | 2s.0d. |
| Two drovers: | 5s.0d. | Swineherd's boy: | 1s.6d. |
| Two other | | Master brewer: | 2s.0d. |
| drovers: | 4s.0d. | His three boys: | 3s.0d. |
| Manure carter: | 2s.0d. | Abbey gardener: | 3s.0d. |
| Cowman: | 2s.0d. | His boy: | 1s.0d. |
| Shepherd: | 2s.0d. | Wood-chopper: | 3s.0d. |
| Lackey: | 1s.6d. | Miller: | 2s.6d. |
| Carter: | 2s.6d. | His boy: | 1s.0d. |

Others received vegetables, loaves and other perquisites for services rendered. 'Obedientiaries' or monastic officials included the Chamberlain, Sacristan, Cantor, Pittancer, Infirmerer and Almoner whose gross income was in another league and totalled £169.2s.6d. Food went with the job. The Abbey's manor farms were responsible for regular supplies of ducks, geese, capons, hens and eggs. The contemporary list of these manors comprised Wyke, Bradford Abbas, Stowell (Somerset), Thornford, Corscombe, Halstock, Oborne, Stalbridge, Stalbridge Weston and Littleham (Devon).

The century saw angry disputes between the monks and the townspeople over joint use of the Abbey Church for monastic and parish purposes. As a result, until the Reformation, there was a permanent partition at the west end of the present church and the Norman building further to the west became All Hallows Parish Church. Its first vicar in 1333 was Hugh le Vycary.

Including these in a fuller contemporary list of the town's churches, chapels and religious institutions shows the extent to which this was an ecclesiastical town: Abbey Church of St Mary the Virgin (Benedictine monastery); All Hallows (Parish Church); St Andrew; St Emorentia; St John the Baptist (Almshouse), St John the Baptist (Hermitage) and St Thomas the Martyr. There were a further two chapels at Sherborne Castle and a parish church in Castleton village.

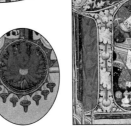

*Illuminations from the Sherborne Missal.*

# Newland

Above: *Dating from the fifteenth century, the Manor House in Newland was re-fronted in about 1820 in Gothic-revival style, and is now the offices of West Dorset District Council and Sherborne Town Council.*

Left: *Detail of the Manor House doorway, its late medieval oriel removed and reset here in the early-nineteenth century, from an eastern gable.*

Above: *The south front of the Manor House, from the south-west, showing an oriel projecting above the doorway.*

Right: *Looking up to the oriel and its window, which adds an elegant touch to the Manor House offices.*

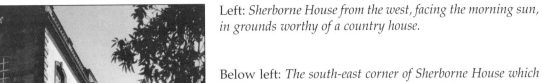

Left: *Sherborne House from the west, facing the morning sun, in grounds worthy of a country house.*

Below left: *The south-east corner of Sherborne House which had its literary heyday in the time of Shakespearean actor William Charles Macready who brought Dickens, Thackeray and Pollock to Sherborne.*

Bottom: *Sherborne House, from the south-east, showing the 1720-built classical frontage of the building which was created by Henry Seymour Portman as a staging-post between his main estates at Bryanston in Dorset and Orchard Portman in Somerset.*

Right: *Sherborne House, behind a high wall on the north side of Newland, during its time as Lord Digby's School.*

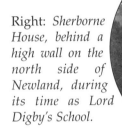

*Westwards along the north side of the street from the junction of Newland with North Road (right).*

Above: *Eighteenth and nineteenth-century houses along the north side of Newland, eastwards from Wembley (left) to Newland Antiques (right) in 1984.*

Top right: *Eastwards along the south side of Newland, from its junction with Cheap Street, with Georgian houses and offices at both ends of this terraced section.*

Below: *Opposite Fosters, looking north-west along the central section of Newland, between North Road (left) and the Avenue (to the right).*

# Eleven

### ⚜

# Fifteenth Century

The vicar of All Hallows Church, in 1400, was William Dalton. He was succeeded by John Campden in 1401. Parishioners appearing before Dean John Chandler, on his second visitation from Salisbury, on 9 October 1408, were Thomas Hilary of Long Street, Robert Gore, John Noblet of the Green, John Livedon of Hound Street, Henry Panter and attorney William Ryder. They produced a long inventory of its chalices, cups, crosses, chasubles and other possessions. Chandler described the condition of 'the prebendal Church of St Mary, Sherborne, with its chapelries', of which that at Pinford was in a state of dilapidation. The chapels at Oborne, 'founded in honour of St Cuthbert', and St Mary Magdalene 'next the castle' were held by John Stokes as vicar. The roof of the latter was in poor repair but it was the Abbot of Sherborne, as patron and rector, who was responsible for upkeep.

On his next visit, on 14 June 1412, Dean Chandler told parishioners that they must repair the roof of the south aisle of All Hallows Church. He received a personal petition from widow Alice Carver, who was given probate over the estate of her late husband, John Carver, who is said to have hidden his will. Isabella Poterne, who separated from her husband, was told to return to him within three weeks or face excommunication.

Dating from the turn of the fifteenth century, the handwritten *Sherborne Missal* is the largest and most lavishly illustrated British book to have survived the Reformation. An illuminated Mass book, setting out services for the year in the finest English Gothic style, it was described in Parliament in 1998 as 'the most important medieval manuscript in the country.' The Arts Minister announced that the Treasury had accepted it in lieu of death duties so that it could remain on display in the British Library. Comprising 690 pages of vellum, it is 15 inches wide by 22 inches down the page, with some 40,000 lines of text, and weighs almost 50lbs. Its future had been in doubt after family and fiscal tragedies hit its owning family, the Dukes of Northumberland, at Alnwick Castle.

The creator of the *Sherborne Missal*, working in the buildings attached to Sherborne Abbey, was a skilled scribe who would have managed a line every few minutes for a six-day week, in a project that must have taken him a minimum of ten months if he had been able to work on it without a break. That would have been spread between 1396 and 1406. John Whas, the Benedictine scribe, signed the *Missal* in four places and records that he did indeed work long

at each daily stint: 'John Whas, the monk, this book's transcription undertaking,/With early rising found his body sorely aching.' He records the feast days of local saints and that of the dedication day of the Abbey Church:

*8 January – St Wulfsin (Bishop Wulfisge III of Sherborne adopted Benedictine rules in 998).*
*23 January – St Emerenciana, Virgin and Martyr (stoned to death Rome, in the catacombs, while praying at the tomb of St Agnes; her church in Sherborne being at Nethercombe).*
*28 April – Translation of St Wulfsin.*
*25 May – St Aldhelm (first Bishop of Sherborne in 705).*
*13 July – St Juthware, Virgin and Martyr (Anglo-Saxon pilgrim, decapitated at Halstock).*
*18 July – Dedication of the Church of St Mary, Sherborne.*

As for the illustrations, which are so numerous that a British Library spokesman told the author that they were 'uncounted if not uncountable', most of these are the work of Dominican friar John Sifer who was regarded as 'the greatest of English limners' (illuminators) and has the credit for having painted the first English self-portrait. There are indeed thousands of 'miniatures' throughout the manuscript, and some 70 coats-of-arms, including those of the King of England and the Prince of Wales, being Richard II and Henry IV who succeeded him in 1399. Secular themes run in parallel with the religious, giving us detailed depictions of feasting, jousting, playing and sleeping. All humanity and life is there, in the full spectrum from saints to sinners, knights to peasants, priests to hermits, birds to beasts. Moses receives the Ten Commandments, Christ sends forth his disciples, and of course goes to his Crucifixion.

The project was sponsored by Richard Mitford, Bishop of Sherborne, and Robert Bruning, Abbot of Sherborne. It is assumed that the *Missal* remained in Sherborne at the Reformation but was then smuggled to safety in France. It first surfaced in a collection of a controller-general of finance for Louis XVI, who was exiled to England at the start of the French Revolution, in 1787.

Once it had returned to Britain, it was acquired by Hugh Percy, 2nd Duke of Northumberland (1742–1817), in 1800 for £215, and remained in Alnwick Castle until recent times. Then, during its period of loan to the British Library, the 11th Duke died of an accidental overdose of drugs in 1996. As a result his brother, Ralph George Algernon Percy, became 12th Duke of Northumberland in what was an unplanned succession, either emotionally or fiscally, to what he described as 'a massive inheritance tax liability' that threatened the integrity of the family's 120,000-acre estate.

After a year, negotiations for the nation to write off the nearly £10 million debt in exchange for the *Missal* appeared to have reached deadlock, until arts correspondent Dalya Alberge exposed in *The Times* the scandal that otherwise the manuscript would have to be sold – probably for well in excess of the figure under debate – and, almost inevitably, to a foreign buyer. The Government was shamed into an almost instant intervention and the deal was done. The *Missal* was saved: for London if not Sherborne. The last word, however, has to go to a correspondent in *The Times*, who pointed out that at no time in these discussions had anyone mentioned its return to those who were the rightful owners, namely the Benedictine Order of the Catholic Church.

As well as illuminated words, architecture was also on the monastic mind though the aspirations of Abbot Brunyng, after 1415, were not realised during his period which ended in 1436. He had hoped to see fashionable Perpendicular lines replacing the Norman fabric.

The monks were still having their differences with the townspeople. There may well have been a period of peace but Abbot Bradford, installed in 1436, revived the power struggle from the previous century by insisting that residents were baptised in his font in the Abbey rather than in their own font in All Hallows Church. In 1437 the argument turned to violence and Sherborne Abbey was torched by an irate cleric with a bow and arrow. It was still the talk of the town when John Leland compiled his Itinerary:

*A priest of All Hallows shot a shaft with fire into the top of that part of St Mary's Church that divided the east part that the monks used from that which the townspeople used; and the partition chancing at that time to be thatched in the roof was set afire and consequently all the whole church, the lead and bells melted, was defaced.*

Flames and heat from the burning roof turned the Ham stone of the higher capitals and their arches from a golden yellow into sunset shades of pink and red. There was also violence in All Hallows where 'the stout butcher' Walter Gauler 'clean defaced the font-stone'. In Sherborne Abbey the legacy of the dispute is the lavish fan-vaulting of the nave and the magnificent choir that replaced their damaged predecessors by the end of the Bradford administration in 1459.

There is also an abundance of smaller details from this period. In the choir of the Abbey, later rescued and returned after being 'negligently stored'

in a side chapel in the eighteenth century, is a finely carved oak relief on one of the miserere seats. The dramatic carving shows a master flogging a boy while he is held across his knees, with a birch across exposed buttocks, while other pupils look on. The character administering the beating wears a round cap rather than a monk's cowl. He could therefore be Thomas Copeland, *'magister scholarum'* of Cheap Street, who donated 3s.4d. towards the foundation of Sherborne Almshouse in 1437. The restoration of Sherborne Abbey continued under Abbot Saunder, between 1459 and 1475, and his successor, Peter Ramsam, who remained in post until 1504.

The Almshouse of Saints John the Baptist and John the Evangelist is on the corner of Trendle Street and Half Moon Street. It is probably on the site of the hospital of the Benedictine monks and indeed its licence from Henry VI, granted to Robert Neville, the Bishop of Sarum, and other worthies in 1437, is for a 'Hospital'. Its chapel and dining hall are of 1438-48, with additional buildings of 1866 to the rear. The original medieval building is as complete as any almshouse in the West of England and follows the plan of a monastic infirmary. Fragments of original stained glass in the south window of the chapel include representations of the two patron saints, with John the Baptist holding the symbolic lamb.

*The earliest part of the Almshouse beside Trendle Street – now its dining-room – dates from between 1438 and 1448 and is seen from the south-east.*

*Fifteenth-century oak screen of the Almshouse Chapel.*
Below: *Almshouse resident Henry Poulter who died there on 7 August 1920.*

National Heritage fund moneys have ensured the retention in the chapel of the Sherborne Triptych, the centrepiece of the painting showing the Raising of Lazarus, which is an outstanding work of the Cologne school of the late 1400s. It probably came to the Almshouse when it was new. Outside, there is a line of mitre-headed bollards in Trendle Street. These cast-iron posts of the 1860s support the rails along the Almshouse pavement. The mitre was the house badge.

At the time of writing, the Almshouse Trust caters for 14 inhabitants. Various rules have been relaxed and attendance at chapel and Abbey services is no longer compulsory. Coming from Sherborne is not a requirement for entry. Neither is the wearing of the Almshouse uniform. Indeed, it is extinct; a photograph is the only memory of the blue blazers for men and red cloaks for women, made in the town by Lowman Bros, the tailors. We do live in dull times.

Their dress was described to the author in 1973 by Victor Swatridge, a Sherborne policeman of the 1920s:

*All the residents wore distinct dress, the men in dark blue uniform, the tunic was belted, with tall crowned hats adorned with a 'cockade'. The ladies were exquisitely dressed in spacious flowing black skirts with hems reaching the ground, frilly blouses over which was draped large coloured woollen shawls and for out-door wear – picturesque pook bonnets tied with ribbon underneath the chin to prevent them being blown off in the wind. Every day these grand old folk walked slowly and stately in procession to the abbey for a short service of divine worship – it was a delightful scene.*

After the death of Sir Stephen Derby, the Julian Hospice facing the Green was inherited by his daughter, Dame Margaret Gough. In 1437 she gave it to the Almshouse as part of its endowment and by 1446 it was 'la Julian's Inn'. It was named for the Benedictine anchoress and mystic Juliana, St Julian of Norwich (1343–1443) whose *Sixteen Reflections of True Love* are still quoted today.

Tenements northwards, along Higher Cheap Street, were owned by the rector of the hospice. The immediate next-door building, the George Inn, has an integral arch under which George Street turns towards Fairfield. It was in use as a hostelry at least as early as 1459 when Richard Coot and John Osteler, from the George Inn, were fined for selling overpriced hay and oats.

Sherborne Abbey, the grandest piece of architecture in Dorset, is largely constructed with the finest available stone which came from ten miles to the west on Hamdon Hill in Somerset. Despite this, it was the local Sherborne stone – also yellowish-brown and also oolitic limestone – that was used after 1539, the year of the suppression of the monastery, for repairs and restoration. Most of the local stone was used in the external walls and Sherborne's late historian, Joseph Fowler, listed the principal changes in his booklet *The Stones of Sherborne Abbey* in 1938.

He draws particular attention to the local stone in the high gabled end of the north transept and the north wall of Bishop Roger's Chapel 'where the flat Norman buttresses and stringcourse are the only Ham stone details left.' On the south side of the Abbey there has been extensive use of Sherborne stone 'to patch and restore the walls and buttresses'. The west end of the Abbey is now almost entirely covered with local stone.

The town of Sherborne is itself largely built with this stone which came from the hillside north of the town where disused quarries can be seen on Charlock Hill, on both sides of the Sandford Road, Clatcombe Farm, Redhole Lane and Nethercombe. The stone was from the top beds of the upper inferior oolite and is a biscuit colour somewhat duller than Ham stone. The 'gooseberry bed' was so called because of the shape and size of its fossils of *Sphoeroidothyris sphaeroidalis* and provided fine blocks of ashlar. The method of extraction was simple as the dry valleys north of Sherborne cut through the stone formations. There was no need to remove overburden and dig pits in the rock: the valleys did this for the quarrymen. Stone was removed directly from the exposed hillside and the vertical working face that resulted moved deeper into the hill as the quarry expanded.

These are linear quarries that follow the edge of the hill. As a result, a single working face extends continuously from Nethercombe to Clatcombe where the top beds were conveniently tilted and would be worked from the surface from the top to the bottom of the valley side. Beside Sandford Lane the quarrymen have left sheer cliffs of yellow stone that stand vertically above green fields. The depth of the quarries at Redhole Lane reached 30 feet.

John Dogget, who was born in Sherborne, was the nephew of Cardinal Bourchier. By 1475 he had advanced to 'the stall of Chardstock in the county of Dorset and the church of Sarum.' Chardstock parish was transferred to Devon in 1844. Dogget continued his advancement and was elected Provost of King's College, Cambridge, in 1499.

Officially known as the Michaelmas Fair, in medieval documents, Pack Monday Fair is said to have been given its popular title by Peter Ramsam, Abbot from 1475 to 1504. It has been ascribed to the 'packing-up day' when workmen gathered their tools on completing the Abbey nave. This is probably purely coincidental. It is likely that the same applied each season as construction used to be summer work, with frosts and short daylight hours preventing year-round progress, and marking the time when travelling bands of masons and carpenters dispersed for home. Michaelmas began the farming year and a more convincing explanation of the 'Pack' name is that it was a hiring fair when labourers made their 'Pact' with new employers.

The choice of date survived the reform of the calendar as it continues to be set for the first Monday after old Michaelmas Day (11 October). Its association with Teddy Roe's Band, the 'rough music' procession through Sherborne at midnight before Pack Monday Fair, is also said to have originated as a noisy celebration of Abbey craftsmen during the Middle Ages.

As well as the survival of the building itself, their work continues to reappear elsewhere, as walls inside older buildings in the town are removed or renovated. This was the case with a fifteenth-century stone statue of the risen Christ, portrayed in relief on a rectangular panel. It was rediscovered in 1987 at the Plume of Feathers, where it had been set horizontally in a wall, during building work.

Undercurrents in Sherborne life were brilliantly captured by Joseph Fowler when he set about a lifetime's work transcribing and translating the town's ecclesiastical and secular records. The possessions of felons were regularly confiscated by the Church. Here, once again, there was scope for argument as the Bishop of Salisbury held rights to the Court of the Hundred in the surrounding countryside which included nine manors owned by the Abbot of Sherborne. The 'Lord of the Liberty of Sherborne' was the Bishop of Salisbury.

Public responsibilities started at an early age with 12-year-old boys being sworn into 'a frankpledge, by statute' as members of their tithing. Offences included keeping unruly dogs, allowing pigs to stray into the town, throwing dung, dumping rubbish, failing to maintain fences, letting hedges overhang paths and ditches overflow across the King's highway.

One of the more esoteric cases concerned John Rickman, accused on 6 May 1483 of 'unjustly, suspiciously, and continuously standing outside his neighbours' doors and windows to listen and learn what they were talking about inside.' He was fined 3d. The date is significant as it was a month into the short reign of the boy-King Edward V who some say was deposed and murdered along with his brother, the Duke of York, in the Tower of London.

Street fighting was commonplace in Sherborne. The usual weapons were fists, sticks and stones but sometimes pitchforks were deployed. Such affrays were beyond the control of the authorities but personal and private attacks could be taken more seriously. John Spencer 'drew blood' in attacking Henry Horsey with a candlestick (fined 9d.). Agnes Broude hit John Loveridge with a porringer (fined 3d.). Thomas Helyer from Abbot's Fee tithing in the centre of Sherborne admitted conniving to enable the escape of a felon in 1487 (fined 6s.8d.). In 1495, Thomas Davy served oaten 'horse-bread' to his hospice patients, rather than loaves intended for human consumption (fined 6d.). John Hill and John Palmer of Overcombe tithing 'ploughed the common way' (they were given 'a love day' in which to put the matter right).

# Sherborne Almshouse

Above: *The Almshouse* (left), *looking southwards, from the cottages of Church Close* (right).

Left: *Original south front of the Almshouse* (left) *with its 1442-dated Chapel* (centre right).

Right: *The fifteenth-century Sherborne Almshouse, in a Victorian print, showing its design based upon that of a medieval monastic infirmary.*

Left: *Detail of the eastern side of the Almshouse from its original Chapel and south wing* (left) *around to present rooms in a nineteenth-century extension* (right).

Right: *East-facing frontage of the Almshouse from Half Moon Street* (foreground) *with Trendle Street at the side* (left) *and the Public Weighbridge House* (near right).

Below: *North wing of the Almshouse facing Church Close.*

Below right: *Mitre-headed bollard – the badge of the Almshouse – beside the building in Trendle Street, dating from the 1860s.*

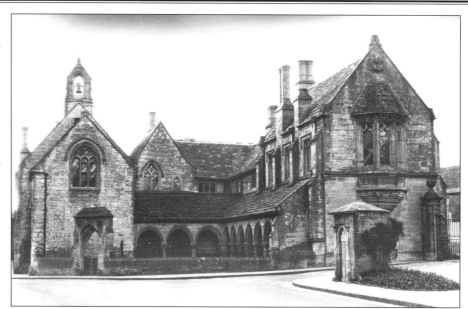

**This image:** *The medieval southern wing of the Almshouse* (right), *in a view westwards from Half Moon Street, into Trendle Street* (centre).

# Twelve

## ❧

# Sixteenth Century

Taking stock of the completed structure of Sherborne Abbey in the final decades of the monastic era, Joseph Fowler listed its building stones and their period in a lecture to the Friends of Sherborne Abbey on 24 March 1938. 'Sherborne Abbey is essentially a Ham Hill Stone building,' he told his audience. 'There is no need to point out which it is, for the whole church, inside and out, from the pinnacles downward, is built of Ham Hill Stone.' All but the earliest pieces of this stone are of the golden limestone, which we know as Ham stone, from the quarries between Stoke-sub-Hamdon and Montacute in Somerset:

*Ham Hill Stone – St Aldhelm's Doorway (of grey bottom-bed Ham stone) and upper part of old Font and stone coffin (10th or 11th c); all Norman work (12th c); and all Perpendicular work (15th c).*
*Tufa – Nave and Choir roof vaulting (15th c).*
*Purbeck Marble – Shaft in Lady Chapel and Abbots' tombs (13th c); lower part of old Font (15th c).*
*Forest Marble – Window shafts in Bishop Roger's Chapel (13th c); later used in replacement steps to Altar and entrance to Chancel (19th c) and shafts in the restored Lady Chapel (20th c).*
*Sherborne Limestone – Exterior walls and parts of buttresses (16th c onwards).*
*Keinton Stone (known as Keinton Marble) – Floor in Ambulatory and steps at south and west Entrances (19th c); floors in Lady Chapel and Bow Chapel (20th c).*
*Purbeck Stone – Replaced Victorian encaustic tiles in the Choir (1963).*

Sherborne Abbey has the heaviest peal of eight bells in the world. The largest of these, the tenor, weighs 46 hundredweight, 5 pounds, and can claim to be one of the seven bells from Tournay, Belgium, which the statesman Cardinal Thomas Wolsey (1475–1530) presented to English churches in 1514. Wolsey had Sherborne connections from his time as a Somerset rector, of Limington near Yeovil, at the start of his career from 1500 to 1503. The 'Great Bell' still carries his name. Removed and re-cast over the winter of 1865–66, it was again re-cast – to B flat – in the 1933–34 partial restoration of the Sherborne bells. It bears the inscription:

*By Wolsey's gift.*
*I measure time for all,*
*To grieve,*
*to church I serve to call.*

The schoolmaster at Sherborne was paid £1 from the parish purse in 1523 'for the keeping of the organs for the whole year.' Another item, in 1534, shows 4s.9d. being paid to John Young for an altar cloth that the schoolmaster's wife gave to the church. Robert Percy was paying 4d. per year as a token rent, in 1537, for use of a room in Church House for his school. This building is part of the row of shops on the north side of Half Moon Street. As A.B. Gourlay pointed out in 1951, a fifteenth-century caricature and accounting note show that the schoolmaster's costume and address were not that of a monk, and this is supported by the sixteenth-century evidence that he was engaged for work in the Parish Church, was non-celibate, and rented rooms outside the monastic precincts.

There may also have been an educational element inside the Abbey including the use of its library which John Leland recorded as having three books by Adam of Barking who had been its distinguished thirteenth-century author. Leland also recorded that Abbot Mere built the Conduit at the lower end of Cheap Street. John Mere was the penultimate abbot, between 1505 and 1535, and the Ham stone tracery of his 'New Well' matched the former Cloister to the south-west. As the monks' washroom, it had only one entrance, and pipes from the Conduit continued to supply Sherborne School, Half Moon Street and nearby Silk Mills into the nineteenth century.

An additional water-supply was needed. A dispute recorded in an Elizabethan Court Roll, between Robert Horrell at the Abbey Mill and towns-people, shows that under 'ancient use and custom' the Coombe Stream was diverted eastwards from noon on Saturday until midday Sunday to flush the Conduit, and formerly the monastic lavatories, as well as those of nearby houses.

William Howell, 'hermit of Saint John the Baptist', died on 7 November 1538. This marked the end of the ancient church, already derelict, for it was 'now down' when John Leland visited Sherborne in 1540. He gives its location as 'St John by the Mill'.

Buried in Sherborne Abbey is Sir Thomas Wyatt (1503–42) who pioneered the sonnet in England. His own life, however, had its own touches of physical passion. He was, as a boy, the lover of Anne Boleyn, who 'sweetly did me kiss, and softly said, 'Dear heart, how do you like this?''

In 1533, when that was a memory and he had a flowing black beard, a bald head, and vast wealth, Wyatt was appointed a Privy Councillor. He was the perfect gentleman, admitting the pre-marital alliance and successfully walking the tightrope as the head of Henry VIII's diplomatic corps until, in 1541, he was imprisoned for a time whilst the King satisfied himself as to Wyatt's connections with Thomas Cromwell, the beheaded Earl of Essex.

Wyatt was 39 when he suffered a sudden fever whilst passing through Sherborne on the King's business, en route from Falmouth to London. He was taken to Clifton Maybank (ST 576 140) and died there. None of his literary works had been published in his lifetime.

The manuscripts included translations of Petrarch's sonnets, a penitential selection of *Certayne Psalmes* (1549) and, influentially, *Songes and Sonettes* which was published as Richard Tottel's so-called *Miscellany* – in which 96 out of a total of 310 are credited to Sir Thomas Wyatt. His memorial at Sherborne reads:

> *In memory of Sir Thomas Wyat* (sic)*, poet and statesman, who died at Clifton Maybank, the house of his friend Sir John Horsey, 11th Oct. 1542 and was buried in the vault in this chapel.*

That was in the north transept but the monument has since been moved, in the spirit of its lines:

> *Wyat resteth here,*
> *that quick could never rest.*

Sir John Horsey (died 1546) of Clifton Maybank, a former *villegiatura* residence of Sherborne Abbey, was its lay impropriator. He became the major beneficiary of the suppression of the Benedictine monastery. It was one of the largest of the 616 religious houses dissolved in England by Henry VIII. As its ex-steward and one of Henry's courtiers he was well placed to take possession and incorporate its lands in his 20,000-acre estate. What saved Sherborne Abbey after the departure of Abbot John Barnstaple and his monks in 1539 was that Horsey sold the great church to the townspeople in 1540 for 100 marks, allowing them to move into it from All Hallows next door and adopt it as their Parish Church. Both Horsey and his son, also Sir John Horsey (1546–64), have their monuments in its north transept. The latter's son was the third Sir John Horsey (1564–89).

Having become redundant, the Norman towers and most of the walls of All Hallows Parish Church were demolished, leaving jagged remains projecting from the west wall of Sherborne Abbey. Its reduced north wall forms the northern side of Abbey Close. The site of All Hallows, now under tarmac and turf, was in use as a graveyard from 1555–1856.

Meanwhile, though parting with buildings, the Horsey family added more ecclesiastical lands – also bought from the Crown – to their property portfolio. They included the manor of Primsley, on Dancing Hill, and that of Pinford towards Goathill and Milborne Port. These were acquired in 1543.

As a result of the Reformation, in 1542, Sherborne was transferred from the see of Salisbury to the new Bristol diocese. The Crown took control of Sherborne Castle and its estate. John Leland, in his Itinerary, mentions the final phase of ecclesiastical building at the Old Castle:

> *One Bishop Langeton made of late time a new piece of work and lodgings of stone at the west end of the haul* [drawbridge]; *other memorable work was none set up since the first building.*

In 1542, in an arrangement uninterrupted by the closure of Sherborne Abbey, secular schoolmaster Robert Percy was still renting his room in Church House. The present Sherborne School inside the old Abbey buildings was founded on 13 May 1550, with letters patent granted by Edward VI, and appears to have had William Gybson, a Fellow of Trinity College, Cambridge, as its first master. Among its benefactors, on his death in 1560, was the former Abbot Barnstaple who had continued to serve the community, as rector of Stalbridge.

Emma Elliott, a widow, found herself in trouble at Primsley Manorial Court in 1563. She farmed the Slopes and had failed to mend her barn (£1 fine, plus further £20 penalty if not repaired) at what is now Limekiln Farm and was responsible for mending gapped hedges and blocked ditches on Dancing Hill (£6.13s.4d. penalty, if not repaired by the Feast of the Annunciation). The work was not done and Mrs Elliott died in 1564. As a result, her horse (valued at £1.13s.4d.) was confiscated and a cash penalty (£6.13s.4d.) levied against her estate, on behalf of the lord of the manor.

Rents and taxes are always with us, and despite the abolition of the office of Abbot of Sherborne there was still a Bishop of Salisbury to be paid. Rent collector Hugh Meyer gives us some idea of the comparable sizes of the boroughs of Newland and Castleton in the 1560s. From Newland he collected £2.6s.4d. whereas the bailiff at Castleton only contributed £1.2s.7d. to the episcopal purse.

Left: *Effigy of Sir John Horsey* (left) *who died in 1546, after turning the Abbey into Sherborne Parish Church, with his son who died in 1564.*

Former monastic rights, such as the Monk's Pathway to Back Lane, were regarded by their new owners as private paths. Widow Ashleigh, whose name survived for the rest of the millennium with the house name Ashleigh's Elm, successfully resisted the imposition of a charge and was 18 years in arrears with her payments in 1575.

'Door silver' was the contemporary rent-book entry for a silver sixpence imposed for the use of a gate on to this and other alleyways that crossed the town. Until the advent of piped water they were 'ways of necessity' as far as the tenants were concerned.

Sherborne School and the Digby Estates Office thought otherwise, successfully resisting centuries of effort at turning them into rights of way. The only exception, in the centre of the town, was Finger Lane which made the transition into a public footpath and links Abbey Road with Acreman Street.

Castleton, the parish that surrounds Sherborne town, began as Castle Farm (ST 647 169) on the edge of the meadows north of the castle ridge. Castletown village grew up north-west of the Old Castle precincts. From Castle Farm, through the farmyard, a road went southwards to the Parish Church (ST 647 168) and then crossed the River Yeo at Dinney Bridge (ST 645 166) before passing to the west of the original Sherborne Lodge (ST 649 165) and heading south-west to Home Farm and Gainsborough Hill. Dinney Bridge has medieval double arches. It was widened in Tudor times but still displays Norman stonework when seen from the water.

North-eastwards from the Parish Church of St Mary Magdalene, skirting the castle slopes, another highway led to Pinford and Tinker's Cross between Milborne Port and Goathill. Both these roads have since lost their public rights. Oborne Road was left as the only through route and thatched Turnpike Cottage takes its name from Doghouse Lane Gate. This was superseded by Pathway Cottage (ST 651 177), half a mile north-east between Blackmarsh Farm and Oborne Chapel, after the present route of the A30 had been dynamited through Crackmore Rocks (ST 667 184).

Before these changes, at the instigation of the Digby family to take the public out of their park, Castleton was a busy place. By 1570 it had seven inns, plus several other beer-houses, a number of mills, and numerous dwellings. Raleigh House, Middle House and Lattice House comprise the only surviving post-medieval terrace at Castleton, in the road west towards the junction beside the former Black Horse Hotel. Lattice House is reputedly the most haunted home in Sherborne. This may have its origins in the belief that in secular hands the Sherborne lands were cursed. King Stephen purloined them and lost his prosperity. They went to the Montague family who lost their male line. Soon after they passed to the Duke of Somerset who was

decapitated. Queen Elizabeth later misappropriated the estate, giving it to a patriotic seaman who would also lose his head, her favourite mariner Sir Walter Raleigh (1552–1618).

'The procession of Queen Elizabeth' hangs in the Red Drawing-Room at Sherborne Castle. It is a huge canvas and an appropriate treasure, for the castle owes its existence to her gift of the Sherborne lands to Raleigh. Broadwindsor's seventeenth-century historian, Thomas Fuller, has in his *Worthies of England* a nice little story – almost certainly untrue but still nonetheless worth telling – that Raleigh had scratched with a diamond on a palace window: 'Fain would I climb, yet fear to fall.' To which Elizabeth is said to have added: 'If the heart fails thee, climb not at all.' In his twenties Raleigh dressed up to the nines in the most magnificent high fashion. His visual presence and style were coupled with the verbal dexterity of a 'bold and plausible tongue'.

In 1584 Raleigh was knighted and the following year Elizabeth prevented him from leaving on the expedition that he had inspired and organised, the attempt at founding a colony to which the Queen had personally given the name Virginia, somewhere on the east coast of North America. Raleigh never did see America and therefore his fame rests upon proxies, particularly his servant Thomas Harriot who brought back to England sacks of potatoes and tobacco and wrote in 1588 a *Brief and True Report of Virginia* which describes how the natives used them. Some of the potatoes found their way into Raleigh's garden at Youghal and thereon rooted themselves as the mainstay of the Irish diet. The tobacco became high fashion because Raleigh adopted it to enhance his flamboyant persona and encouraged fellow courtiers to copy his example.

In 1588, Elizabeth found a new favourite, Robert Devereux, 2nd Earl of Essex, and Raleigh fell from grace when the Queen discovered he was having an affair with one of her maids, Elizabeth Throgmorton. The pair spent a few weeks in the Tower of London and he was then released conditionally, as what he called the 'Queen of England's poor captive', to sort out the distribution of the £150,000 prize-money – the bulk of it going to the Queen – when the great carrack, the *Madre de Dios*, was brought into Dartmouth. It was sufficient service for the Queen to give Raleigh his freedom but he was to be banished from the royal court for four years.

Raleigh married Elizabeth Throgmorton and in January 1592 he bought a 99-year lease on the Old Castle and its park at Sherborne. He put his efforts into repairing the castle, but tired of persistent mould on his clothes, books and other possessions. It was the impossibility of beating the damp that caused him to abandon the improvements to the Old Castle in 1594 and to set about building a modern four-storey home where the early-Tudor hunting lodge stood – on the rise a quarter of a mile to the south of the Old Castle (ST 649 165).

Dressed stone for the four towers and Dutch-style curves to the top of the façade came from Ham Hill and the curtain wall of the Old Castle was used for the main rubble of the walls. Their general roughness caused the need for plastering, which was then an exceedingly uncommon building technique. Indeed, it is one of the earliest plastered houses in the land. It was also an unusually light house, having leaded-glass windows that took up a large proportion of the available wall space, though most of these were considerably reduced or totally blocked during the subsequent expansion of the house.

### Sherborne New Castle

Sherborne Lodge, as the New Castle was first called, perpetuated the name of the hunting lodge it had replaced, but gradually it became known as Sherborne Castle (or Sherborne New Castle to try to avoid the inevitable confusion with the Old Castle), although it is not a castle at all and would have been impossible to defend with so many ground-floor windows. The Keep of the Old Castle was retained as state rooms for entertaining; the one thing for which it was perfectly suited was medieval banquets and in it the guests could be given free rein. Adrian Gilbert, Raleigh's half-brother, was installed there as the bailiff.

Some rooms of the New Castle had austere plastering, but others were panelled in oak, and tapestries were hung in the first-floor salon which has a superb fireplace and an ornate moulded-plaster ceiling which features the Raleigh coat of arms.

Tree planting was carried out extensively and the last of the great cedars are as old as any in England, having been brought back for Raleigh by his captains from the North American expeditions. Raleigh's Grove survives and below it he had elaborate water-gardens, neat hanging terraces, a bowling-green, and fruit orchards.

Thomas Harriot, who had brought Europe its tobacco and potatoes, was given a home. He was a mathematician and a deist, disbelieving that the divine being had manifested himself in Christ. Their unorthodox friends included Christopher Marlowe (1564–93), credited with *The Atheist's Tragedy*. The beautiful lines for which Marlowe is best remembered were dedicated to Walter Raleigh:

> *Come live with me and be my love,*
> *And we will all the pleasures prove.*

They were perceived as a personal invitation to Raleigh and a skit on his imagined responses was produced by Izaac Walton (1593–1683) as *The Nymph's Reply* 'made by Sir Walter Raleigh in his younger days.' Marlowe was stabbed with a death-thrust into his eye during a drunken brawl at Deptford. A warrant was out for his arrest on charges of disseminating irreligious tracts.

On 21 March 1594 Thomas Howard, 3rd Viscount Bindon, was ordered by the Ecclesiastical Commissioners to hold an inquiry at Cerne Abbey into allegations that Raleigh had attended an atheistic lecture delivered by Marlowe. There is no surviving documentation of the outcome of this and

*Sir John Horsey and his merry men* (left) *confronting the Abbot of Sherborne and the Bishop of Salisbury* (centre) *as they prepare to evict the Benedictine monks* (right) *from Sherborne Abbey in the 1905 re-enactment of events in 1539.*

a series of similar accusations. A Catholic pamphleteer of 1592 had denounced 'Sir Walter Rawley's School of Atheism' and claimed its scholars were 'taught among other things to spell God backwards.'

Raleigh, meanwhile, turned his energies to the search for Eldorado. The first expedition, on his behalf, brought back nothing, so on 9 February 1595 he personally led a fleet of five ships out of Plymouth to the South American coast of Guiana. They did find some gold-stained quartz but no fabulous city. The mahogany they brought back was the first to be seen in England.

In 1596 Raleigh was back at Sherborne and in June he commanded the *Warspite* at the head of the English fleet that carried out the storming of Cadiz, in which he narrowly survived severe wounds. Despite various personal animosities, Raleigh was back in public acceptance if not full favour. He was the Member of Parliament for Dorset in 1597 and for Cornwall in 1601 and encouraged West Country boatmen to begin their lucrative trade with the Newfoundland fisheries.

Politics turned against Raleigh on the death of Queen Elizabeth in 1603. James I came to London from Scotland with the belief that Raleigh would oppose him, and though that proved unfounded he was prepared to believe that Raleigh was involved in a 'plot to surprise the king's person'. The evidence against him was feeble, amounting to the fact that he had borrowed a book that refuted James' title to the throne. That he denied, but then had to admit; and he was known to be on friendly terms with the alleged plotters. It was enough for conspiracy convictions at the time, and Raleigh was convicted and sentenced to death on 11 December 1603.

Instead of execution he was sent to the Tower of London. Legal arguments followed over the forfeiture of the Sherborne estate, which from 1608–12 was bestowed upon Robert Carr, Earl of Somerset, but was then bought back by the Crown. Raleigh was able to live in the Tower with his wife and son, and to write his *Historie of the World*. His elegant Elizabethan prose twists into a masterly protest against the Stuart 'divine-right' absolutism that was to claim his head. Meanwhile he was allowed to set up a laboratory in which he desalinated Thames water by distillation.

In March 1616 he was released from the Tower and allowed to prepare another expedition to the Orinoco, in search of gold, on the condition that he

*The south-west gatehouse, from the outside, looking eastwards across what would have been its drawbridge.*

did nothing to harass the Spanish. A fleet of 14 ships sailed from Plymouth on 12 June 1617.

They immediately hit trouble. Storm-force winds caused one to sink and the rest were scattered. Most eventually staggered into Cork for repairs.

They sailed again on 19 August. This time they would languish for 40 days in the doldrums, running short of water and with deaths from fevers and scurvy bringing the crews to the point of mutiny.

Worse followed their arrival on the Venezuela coast. Lawrence Kemys was sent ahead to find the gold mine, and instructed to avoid a confrontation with the Spaniards, but on finding the town of San Tomas in the way, he attacked it and Raleigh's son, Walter, was killed in the process. Raleigh was so distraught at the outcome that Kemys killed himself. The expedition then fell apart, with some of the ships, Raleigh's included, departing for home via Newfoundland.

He returned with fish rather than gold. Even with the latter he would have been in trouble, however, as James had promised the Spaniards that there would be retribution for the unauthorised attack on their settlement. James ordered Raleigh's trial but it was pointed out that this was a legal impossibility as he was already under sentence of death for treason. That was carried out with an axe on the scaffold in Old Palace Yard on the morning of 28 October 1618.

It was with a brave face that Raleigh made his exit. Someone complained that his head should face towards the east as it lay on the block. 'What matter how the head lie,' he answered, 'so the heart be right?'

The living link between the Old Castle and Sir Walter Raleigh is the clove pink which grows in clumps on its banks. Sherborne tradition credits Lady Elizabeth Raleigh with having introduced *Dianthus caryophyllus*, 'Simplex Major', which is known in the town as Lady Betty's Pink. For special occasions, flowers are cut to decorate Leweston Chapel in Sherborne Abbey, where Sir Walter and Lady Betty sat for services.

Court cases in Sherborne towards the end of the century included that concerning James Compton of Overcome, in 1592, who had closed the road to Old Down which prevented access to the stream from which water was customarily collected (fined £2). In 1597, Richard Oringe obstructed and resisted the town constable, John Chetmill, saying 'thou art a rascal knave' (fined £5).

# *Sherborne Abbey*

Above: *Sherborne Abbey, looking north-eastwards across the churchyard from Church Close, in an early-nineteenth-century print.*

Below: *Edwardian view of Sherborne Abbey, from the south-west, showing Anglo-Saxon and medieval walling where All Hallows Parish Church was attached to the main building* (left).

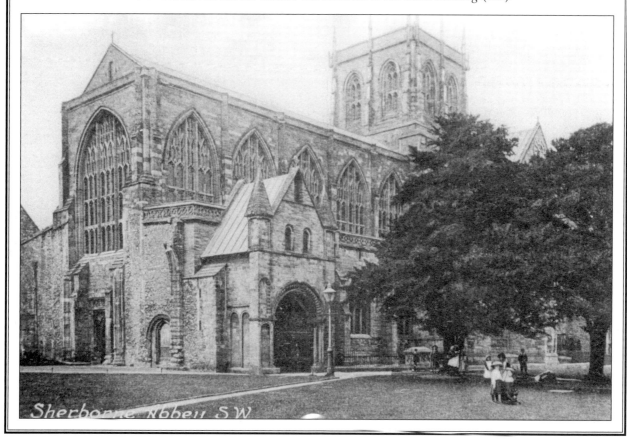

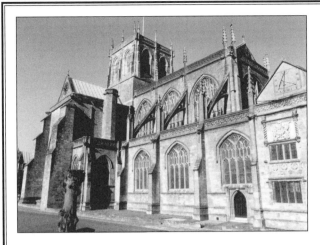

Left: *The south-east frontage of Sherborne Abbey from the south porch* (left) *to the sundial (showing 11 o'clock) above the Chapel of St Mary le Bow* (right).

Below left: *Flying buttresses* (right centre) *linking the twin levels of the south aisle and presbytery towards the eastern end of Sherborne Abbey.*

*Westwards along Church Lane, through Bow Arch, the direct pedestrian access from the town centre to the Abbey.*

Below: *Sherborne Abbey and the roofs of Half Moon Street* (foreground) *from the south.*

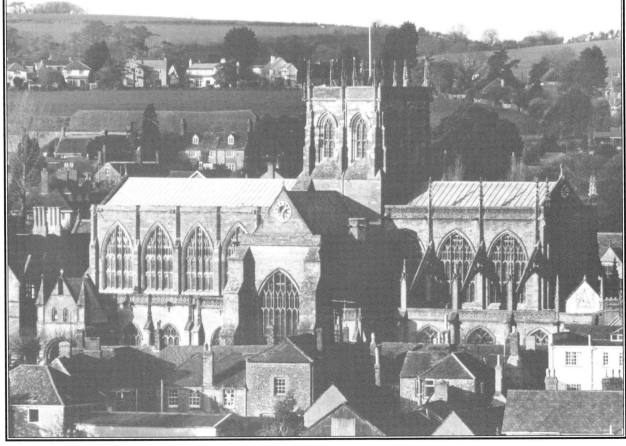

Above: *Sundial* (centre) *above St Mary le Bow Chapel of Sherborne Abbey* (top left), *which housed the first classroom of Sherborne School, in a view over the roofs of Half Moon Street* (foreground) *from the Terrace.*

*Ecclesiastical welcome, in the south porch* (left), *to Sherborne and Dorset's best architecture.*

Above: *Churchyard view from the Abbey approach, north-eastwards through pollarded limes to the Chapel of St Mary le Bow* (centre left), *Church Lane and the 1884-built memorial to George Digby Wingfield Digby* (centre right).

Right: *Fourteenth-century north wall of All Hallows Church.*

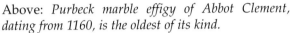

Above: *Purbeck marble effigy of Abbot Clement, dating from 1160, is the oldest of its kind.*

Above right: *Early-thirteenth-century priest in Mass vestments, carved in Purbeck marble.*

Right: *Purbeck marble effigy of an Abbot of Sherborne – probably Laurence de Bradford – decorated with head corbels (foreground and top left).*

Left: *Eastwards from above the south transept, over the south aisle of the Abbey, along Church Lane to Long Street and the former Sherborne Brewery* (centre top), *with Half Moon Street to the south-east* (right).

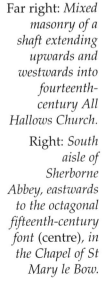

Far right: *Mixed masonry of a shaft extending upwards and westwards into fourteenth-century All Hallows Church.*

Right: *South aisle of Sherborne Abbey, eastwards to the octagonal fifteenth-century font (centre), in the Chapel of St Mary le Bow.*

Top left: *The badge of the Dorsetshire Regiment, in Sherborne Abbey, featuring the Marabout Barracks in Dorchester and the motto 'Primus in Indis' (First in the Indies).*

Above: *Battle honours (centre) and memorials to the county's own regiment.*

Left: *Colours of the Dorsetshire Regiment hanging in Sherborne Abbey.*

Below: *One of the fifteenth-century misericord seats in the choir stalls.*

Left: *Faces of the punished pupil and his master, who may well be Thomas Copeland, as he was Sherborne's 'magister scholarum' in 1437.*

Above: *Misericord seat lifted to reveal its oak-carved classroom scene of a Sherborne schoolmaster birching a boy with other pupils looking on.*

Right: *Central detail of teaching and correction in medieval Sherborne.*

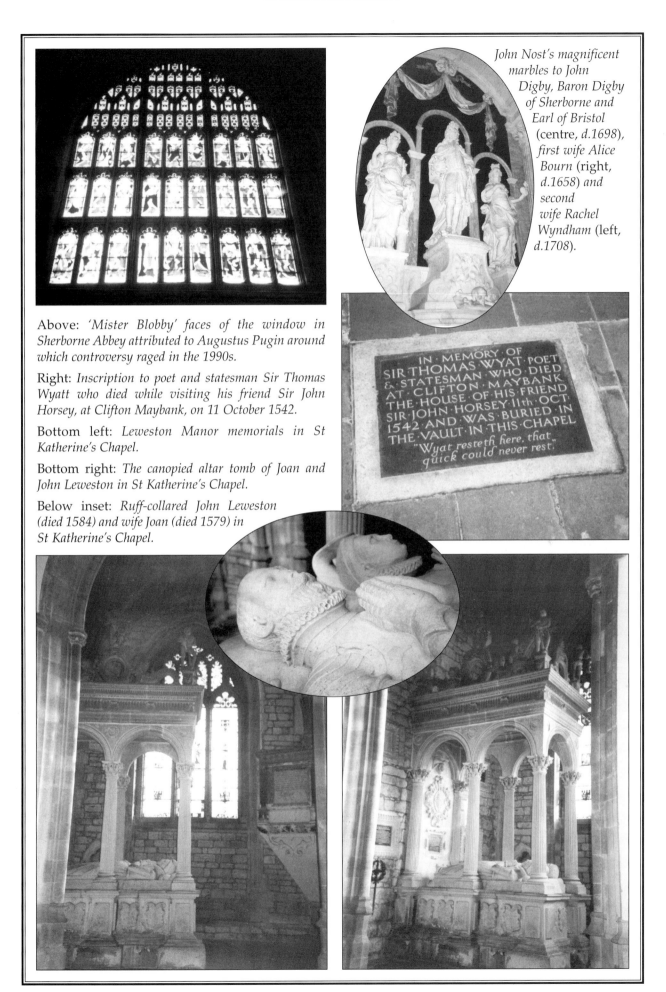

John Nost's magnificent marbles to John Digby, Baron Digby of Sherborne and Earl of Bristol (centre, d.1698), first wife Alice Bourn (right, d.1658) and second wife Rachel Wyndham (left, d.1708).

Above: 'Mister Blobby' faces of the window in Sherborne Abbey attributed to Augustus Pugin around which controversy raged in the 1990s.

Right: Inscription to poet and statesman Sir Thomas Wyatt who died while visiting his friend Sir John Horsey, at Clifton Maybank, on 11 October 1542.

Bottom left: Leweston Manor memorials in St Katherine's Chapel.

Bottom right: The canopied altar tomb of Joan and John Leweston in St Katherine's Chapel.

Below inset: Ruff-collared John Leweston (died 1584) and wife Joan (died 1579) in St Katherine's Chapel.

**Above:** *'Jimmy', a sculpture by Martin Turner, was presented to Sherborne Abbey on Armistice Day in 1999.*

**Above:** *Marble cherubs, above Joan and John Leweston's memorial, with the interlaced vaulting of St Katherine's Chapel.*

**Above:** *The clock mechanism bought new from William Monk of Berwick St Johns for £25 in 1740.*

**Background print:** *The nave of Sherborne Abbey, westwards from the Choir.*

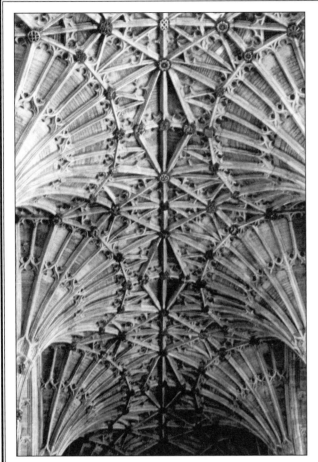

This Monument was erected by
Mr *THOMAS MANSEL* of this Towne,
in Remembrance of a Great Hailſtorme:May.16.A.D.1709
between the hours of one and four in the afternoon;
which ſtopping the courſe of a ſmall River Weſt of
this Church; cauſ'd of a ſudden an Extraordinary Flood
in the Abbey-garden, and Green;
running with ſo Rapid a ſtream,that it forc'd
open the North-door of the Church, diſplac'd,
and remov'd about 7222 foot of the Pavement,
and was 2 foot and 10 Inches high as it paſſ'd
out at this South-Door.

**Top left:** *Soaring view of fan-vaulting and bosses of the best roof in Dorset.*

**Top right:** *Abbey view, east-south-east from the tower, over Church Lane (bottom left) and the junction of Cheap Street with South Street and Half Moon Street (centre left).*

**Above:** *Memorial to a natural event, the 'Great Hailstorm' of 16 May 1709, in Sherborne Abbey.*

**Left:** *Town Hall site and the Eleanor Cross erected in memory of George Digby Wingfield-Digby, in 1884, between Half Moon Street and the south transept of Sherborne Abbey.*

*Late-fifteenth-century Ham stone vault of the nave in Sherborne Abbey.*

# Thirteen

❖

# Seventeenth Century

Though there was probably an earlier chapel in the vicinity, the present Parish Church of St Mary Magdalene at Castleton was built by Sir Walter Raleigh to replace the medieval church in Maudlin's Close, on the north-east side of the Old Castle. Items brought from the previous building included the oak staircase and fifteenth-century font, and there are the later 1671-dated royal arms of Charles II. Raleigh's replacement church has a commemorative stone from 1601 set in the east gable. Pride of place, however, goes to a memorial over the first door which dates from about the time of its rebuilding in 1714. It is to a 96-year-old 'faithful servant to ye Earls of Bristol', Margaret Barnard, who died in 1716.

Raleigh's Seat (ST 647 167) is of monumental stonework on a stepped plinth set into the west wall of Sherborne Park above the River Yeo. Next to it, backing out of sight, is the seat for his servant. Raleigh retreated to this arbour for a quiet smoke and is said to reappear annually on the eve of the Feast of St Michael, which is on 29 September. His ghost walks peacefully through the trees, sits below Raleigh's Oak, and then vanishes. In real life Raleigh sat there and contemplated his next verse.

Better known is the story, probably apocryphal, that it was when he was puffing away in Raleigh's Seat that a servant doused him with ale to put out the fire. The same story is commemorated by the Virginia Ash Hotel in Sherborne Road at Henstridge. In the same corner of Sherborne Park as the famous seat is the cemetery for the Digbys' Keeshond dogs but their memorial stones have been removed.

The town of Sherborn in Massachusetts, settled in 1652, was incorporated as a community in 1674. Monks' Walk Cedars (ST 649 168) on the north-west side of Sherborne Lake are ageing Great Virginia Cedars brought by Raleigh's traders from the New World. Vines were grown on this south-facing slope in medieval times. The monastic connection seems to be modern romanticism.

Raleigh's Sherborne estate, after being bestowed on Robert Carr, Earl of Somerset, was then bought back by the Crown. Raleigh was finally persuaded to sign its surrender in 1614 and it was sold in 1617 to the diplomat Sir John Digby (1580–1653), who paid £10,000 for the Sherborne estates and brought a name to Castleton and Sherborne that flourishes to this day. He had been the British ambassador to Madrid since 1611 and was trying to arrange a marriage between the two crowns of Prince Charles of England with the Infanta Maria of Spain. The proposed match was called off in 1618, because the English monarch James I would not concede liberty of conscience in religion to the country's Roman Catholics.

Digby, however, would be rewarded for his patience and diplomatic skill. He was given a peerage, becoming Lord Digby, and in 1622 he was created Earl of Bristol. When the marriage arrangement failed Digby returned to England and Sherborne Lodge, which in 1625 he proceeded to expand. Four wings were added, three being symmetrical and the other expanded into a banqueting hall which has survived to this day with its oak panelling and internal porches almost unaltered. The new house was to an 'H' plan which was said to have been in honour of Henry, Prince of Wales, the son and heir of James I. The library, on the other hand, is in a wing that was remodelled in the Strawberry Hill Gothic that came into vogue in the mid-eighteenth century. As for Digby's later life, he took the side of Charles I in the Civil War but then disassociated himself from the King's efforts to prolong the struggle. This brought about his enforced exile and it was in Paris that he would die in 1653.

Brave and defiant Lady Lettice Digby (1588–1658), supported by only women and boys, held Geashill Castle against besieging Irish rebels in 1642. Her portrait in Sherborne Castle shows her with a book carrying the scriptural reference that summed up her life, from the Book of Job (xix, 20): 'I am escaped with the skin of my teeth.'

The Old Castle at Sherborne, redundant apart from its Keep which was still in occasional use for banquets, was hastily re-fortified for the cause of King Charles. Its polygonal outworks were strengthened with an outer bastion to the east. Raleigh's new Sherborne Castle was a fortress only in name, and was indefensible, but the Old Castle had been designed to withstand the ebb and flow of marching men. It did so successfully in the first siege of 1642 but the return match in 1645 was another matter. The Commander of the forces raised by Parliament, General Sir Thomas Fairfax, had to waste the efforts of an army to break into the former Bishop's Palace. Oliver Cromwell remarked that this was a 'malicious and mischievous castle – like its owner.'

He was Lord Digby, adviser to the King, and its defence had been organised by his stepson, Sir Lewis Dyve, who held out against a vigorous siege for 16 days. The Old Castle was stormed on 15 August 1645. Among those killed during the siege, though in the service of the Parliamentary Army that was doing the attacking, was Captain John Horsey from the Clifton Maybank family. The third son of Sir George Horsey and Elizabeth Freke, he was a descendant of Sir John Horsey who bought Sherborne Abbey and its lands, via his younger son Jasper Horsey.

As with Corfe Castle in the Isle of Purbeck, the destruction of Sherborne Castle was ordered by the House of Commons. This was completed by October 1646 and Digby was lucky to retain his estate. After the Civil War moved on from Sherborne, in 1648, a bill of 3s.6d. was issued to cover the aftermath; this paid for three days' labour and the 'straw and besoms' required to 'make clean the School after the removing of the soldiers.'

Revd William Lydford was Sherborne's vicar from 1632 when he had been appointed 'at the instance of Lord Digby'. A Puritan, 'upon the commencement of Civil War he espoused the cause of Parliament',

but 'took no active part in the public broils'. On his death in 1653, the townspeople 'did not wait for the Lord Protector or any other patron to select a minister' and took it on themselves to appoint Revd Francis Bampfield, the rector of Rampisham. He left its 'rich living' to respond to 'the call to one of the most populous towns in all Dorsetshire.'

He was the son of Sir John Bampfield of Poltimore, Devon, who represented Penryn in the Long Parliament. His brother was Thomas Bampfield, MP, from Exeter, who was the Speaker of the House of Commons during Richard Cromwell's Protectorate. Clergyman Francis Bampfield became a devout Presbyterian, refusing to use the Prayer Book, and worked a 'reformation in the town in general and was blessed to the conversion of many souls.' He was said to be 'the most celebrated preacher in the West of England, and even beyond

*Right: Sherborne New Castle from the south-east, drawn by John Preston Neale in 1830.*

*Below: The earliest known photograph of Castle Court, in the middle of the Old Castle, by John Pouncy from Dorchester, was published in 1857.*

measure admired by his hearers.' That ended with the Act of Uniformity which caused Francis Bampfield to take leave 'of his sorrowful congregation the Lord's day before Bartholomew Day' in 1662. He was now a Nonconformist, 'preaching the gospel outside the Established Church'. Within weeks, on 19 September 1662, soldiers burst into his house as he was holding a service. Bampfield, his former curate, and 25 parishioners were arrested. All except the clergymen, who were held separately, found themselves incarcerated in a room with only a single bed, at the New Inn, where they were held for five days and nights. The soldiers were then bribed to allow Bampfield to hold a Sunday service for the detainees. The following Wednesday they appeared before Sir John Strode of Parnham House, Beaminster, who committed them on a charge of sedition.

Bampfield was not put off, and went to preach at Dunkerton and Shaftesbury, as a result of which he was imprisoned at Dorchester and held for nine years. A bachelor, he had a loyal female servant who continued to visit him throughout, until scandal spread about them. The minister responded by marrying her, which distressed the Bampfield family, who considered her to be 'beneath him'. On being discharged from Dorchester Gaol, in 1675, he went to Salisbury and London where he founded a conjugation of Sabbatarian Baptists at Pinners' Hall, Broad Street. This had him thrown into Newgate Prison where he wrote *The Lord's Free Prisoner* and died on 16 February 1684.

Bampfield's curate since 1658, Revd Humphrey Phillips (1632–1707), also went on to preach at Dunkerton and Shaftesbury. The cold and damp of Ilchester Gaol, endured for almost a year, required a period of recovery in Holland. Then he threw himself back into the West Country preaching circuit, causing a 'much vexed' Bishop's Court at Wells to declare his excommunication.

Seventeenth-century strife could prove hazardous to all persuasions. Thomas Winniffe, Bishop of Lincoln (1576–1654), was born in Sherborne. He was the son of John Winniffe (1540–1630). Having debated moral philosophy before King James I at Oxford in 1605, Thomas Winniffe became chaplain to Prince Charles in 1622 but was sent to the Tower of London for equating Spinola with the devil. After apologising to the Spaniards he resumed his job and was in post after the accession of King Charles I.

Then Winniffe succeeded John Donne as Dean of St Paul's on 8 April 1631. He then followed John Williams, in Lincoln Cathedral, after he had been promoted to York in 1641. Civil War disturbances led to his house in Westminster being destroyed by a mob led by Sir Richard Wiseman who was killed during the incident. Winniffe was then forced to quit his see at Lincoln, though he 'submitted to all ordinances, and was never charged with delinquency.'

The Civil War had also upset the religious order of things much closer to home. An 'Indulgence' granted by King Charles II in 1672 enabled Humphrey Phillips to return to Sherborne. He took out a licence as a Presbyterian teacher in two houses in the town, owned by Catharine Chaffey and John Copton. Then the homes of Francis Ford and Elizabeth Cooth were similarly licensed. The influential Nonconformist community built him a meeting-house, capable of holding 500 people, but in 1673 the Indulgence was revoked. Phillips was succeeded by Revd Josiah Banger (1627–91), the son of Revd Bernard Banger of Yarlington, Somerset, who was also forced to move on, to Montacute.

Ilchester Gaol then figures in his story, after which Banger moved back to the Sherborne countryside, to the tiny village of Lillington, where he held Sunday services attended by '300 people or above'. During his time James Scott, Duke of Monmouth and illegitimate son of King Charles II, landed at Lyme Regis in the summer of 1685 to claim the Stuart throne from his uncle, James II. After his peasant army was routed at the Battle of Sedgemoor, the Lord Chief Justice, Baron George Jeffreys, brought vengeance in his wake with the judicial retribution of the Bloody Assize.

A dozen of those sentenced to death for supporting the rebellion were sent to Sherborne for execution. Each victim was to be given a traitor's death, to be hanged, drawn and quartered, with the butchery taking place whilst they were still alive. Of those who suffered at Sherborne, Samuel Glisson, Richard Hall and John Savage came from the town.

Nathaniel Highmore, MD (1613–85), the rector's son from Purse Caundle, pushed forward the frontiers of medicine in 1651 with his treatise on the structure of the human body, *Corporis Humani disquisitio anatomica in que sanguinis circulationem prosequuutus est*. In it, he writes of an '*alexipharmaca dispositio vitalium*' which he says enabled a student, when he was at Oxford, to eat spiders with impunity. He relates how the cavity in the superior maxillary, an air pocket in the cheekbone – since known as the 'antrum of Highmore' – was brought to his attention by a lady patient, whose abscess he had drained by removing her left canine. He also writes of dissecting an ostrich. Dr Highmore's surgery was in Sherborne. He is buried inside the church at Purse Caundle, on the south side of the chancel.

The Dutch claimant to the throne, William, Prince of Orange (1650–1702), landed in Tor Bay and set up his temporary headquarters in Sherborne Castle, Castleton – 'The Lodge' built by Sir Walter Raleigh – at the invitation of John Digby, 3rd Earl of Bristol, and his cause gathered the momentum that would make him the next King of England. He received at Sherborne the key defectors from James II's army – Churchill, Grafton, Berkeley, Kirke and Trelawney – and Lieutenant Byng from the King's fleet at Portsmouth who brought the welcome news that the Navy was divided and in no mood for a fight.

Prince George of Denmark rode into Sherborne Park with the Duke of Ormond at about four o'clock on the afternoon of Thursday 29 November 1688. There was much for the Prince of Orange to be pleased about and his propaganda machine went into action. Proclamations were printed at Sherborne, John Hutchins records: 'It is said that his proclamation emanated from a printing press set up in the drawing room, where a broken hearth stone bore to the fact until very recently.'

The spurious 'Third Declaration' issued from 'Sherbun Castle, 28 Nov. 1688' was in fact an over-zealous forgery, compiled by Sir Hugh Speke and making an unauthorised command that Protestants were to disarm and imprison their Catholic neighbours. This edict inflamed the situation in London and led directly to the looting of the capital's Catholic chapels on the night of 21 December 1688, when a mob also broke into the residence of the Spanish Ambassador.

William himself was above street politics. His wide achievement would be to take religion out of politics in England, though in Ireland the position had already irreversibly polarised. The aristocracy who paved the way for this transfer of power by plotting in the ice-house at Charborough Park would protect their own rights through the supremacy of Parliament.

Enduring reform was ensured by the Bill of Rights which reduced the monarch to a non-executive head of state. For William there would be problems in coming to terms with regal responsibility being distanced from power, but in the longer term the Glorious Revolution saved Britain from a bloodier transition of the sort that ended the age of kings in the other great European powers.

For all that the Glorious Revolution would be all but forgotten by most Englishmen. Its lasting emotional peaks were across the water, in the 'No Surrender' of the Londonderry siege and the climactic defeat of James II's army at the Battle of the Boyne on 1 July 1690.

William had become the last English monarch to ride into battle at the head of his army. There, indeed, the Middle Ages were finally brought to a close.

Revd Thomas Curgenven was rector of Folke in the late-seventeenth century but was remembered as a brilliant classical scholar. Not that much of his own work survives, but as master of Sherborne School he skilfully passed on his enthusiasms to a talented new generation. In particular he was instrumental in helping Thomas Creech (1659–1700) to embark upon a career of translating. His assistance is acknowledged in the latter's works on Theocritus and Horace.

Thomas Creech was born at Blandford and sent to Sherborne School. His father, also Thomas, outlived him, and his mother, Jane Creech, died in 1693. They both stayed in Blandford and were proud of a son who became one of Britain's most accomplished translators of the classics from the Greek and Roman world. His *Lucretius* was a best seller.

'Incomparable', it was called. Creech was headmaster of Sherborne School from 1694–96, but then fell in love with Miss Philadelphia Playdell of Oxford, whose parents would not approve of a marriage. Creech's last months were spent in a manic depression and their end is recorded by John Hobson:

*He had prepared a razor and a rope, and with the razor he had nicked his throat a little, which hurt him so much that he desisted; then he took the cord and tied himself up so low that he kneeled on his knees while he was dead.*

His sister, Bridget, was married to Thomas Bastard, the town architect at Blandford. They and the Playdells found themselves the centre of attention as catch penny scandal sheets were printed about the suicide. One such was entitled 'A Step to Oxford, or a Mad Essay on the Reverend Mr Thos Creech's hanging himself (as 'tis said) for love. With the Character of his Mistress.'

Sherborne's charity school, endowed by Richard Foster with the rent from Foster's Farm at Boys Hill, near Holnest, was popularly known as the Blue School. The 'Blue Boys' of charity schools across the land wore blue coats and the name survives in its own right at Blewcoat School in Caxton Street, Westminster. John Foster was the first master, in 1687, and ten pupils formed the initial intake, though by 1696 the rules were relaxed to provide for a dozen boys. The 'house in which Foster's School is held' survives on the south-west corner of Abbey Close.

Having seen the triumph of the Glorious Revolution, Revd Josiah Banger died at Lillington in August 1691, and was succeeded as Sherborne's Dissenting minister by Revd John England. His flock comprised many of the town's artisans whose main work was in high fashion, manufacturing linen buttons for dresses and uniforms.

Otherwise known as the Leweston Chapel, St Katherine's Chapel, at the side of the nave in Sherborne Abbey, contains the bodies of the Winston family from Standish, Gloucestershire, whose main base in Dorset was at Longburton. Sir Henry Winston's daughters included Sarah who married John Churchill from Round Chimneys Farm at Glanvilles Wootton. As the nation's hero he was created the Duke of Marlborough and was later given Blenheim Palace by a grateful people. The family's enduring political dynasty stretched from Winston Churchill of the Civil War period, who married Elizabeth Drake from Ashe, near Axminster, through to Winston Churchill of the last century's darkest hour.

John Digby, 3rd Earl of Bristol, died in 1698. Though he had married two heiresses he left no children and therefore the title died with him. Sherborne Castle passed to a cousin, William Digby, 5th Baron Digby, who had succeeded his brother, Simon Digby, 4th Baron Digby. Other possessions were left to John Digby's sister, Lady Sunderland.

# Sherborne New Castle

Left: *The classic portrait of master-mariner Sir Walter Raleigh in Sherborne Castle.*

Below: *Father Sir Walter Raleigh and son Walter Raleigh – baptised at Lillington, near Sherborne, on 1 November 1593 – painted in 1602.*

Above: *Identical towers either side of the entrance to Sir Walter Raleigh's Sherborne Castle.*

Below: *Sherborne Castle from the south-east, photographed by Colin Graham in 1975.*

*Jerusalem (top left) and the Deer Park east of Sherborne Lake (bottom right).*

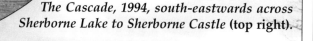

Left: *Functional concrete and steel overflow outlet from Sherborne Lake, built to the south of the Cascade in 1973, to spare the latter and the town from potentially devastating flood damage.*

Bottom left: Ginkgo biloba, *a Palaeozoic tree from 200 million years ago that is the oldest living species in the world, was introduced from China to Utrecht in 1730 and had reached Sherborne Park (this specimen) by 1770.*

**The Cascade, 1994, south-eastwards across Sherborne Lake to Sherborne Castle (top right).**

## Fourteen

## Eighteenth Century

An inscription beside the entrance to Sherborne Abbey records a newsworthy natural event early in the eighteenth century:

*This Monument was erected by Mr Thomas Mansel of this town, in remembrance of a Great Hailstorm, 16 May 1709, between the hours of one and four in the afternoon; which stopping the course of a small river west of this Church caused of [sic] an extraordinary flood in the Abbey garden and Green; running with so rapid a stream, that it forced open the north door of the Church, displaced and removed about 1,222 foot of the pavement, and was 2 foot and 10 inches high as it passed out at this south door.*

The growing number of Nonconformist churches hardly begin to compete when compared to the Abbey's role as a physical repository for the town's collective memory. Revd John England's Dissenting meeting-house was in Newland, with his manse adjoining, and was conveyed to the local Presbyterian trustees by Mary Keynes in 1707. It was 'bounded on the north side by the Quaker's meeting house and burying ground.' Miss Sarah Dampier gave Whetcombe's Close in Acreman Street – later known as Chapel Field – to the 'minister of the congregation of Protestant Presbyterian Dissenters in Sherborne' to 'use the rents and profits' as recompense for his pains in preaching the gospel.'

Silver communion cups were presented by Miss Mary Kelsby in 1723. She had lost her sight at the age of nine. This explains the provision in her will, in which she left Dalwood's House in Cheap Street to the community, for the funding of the distribution of half-crowns to the poor, but with a crown going to those who were blind. Another blind lady, Miss Grace Downing Scott, did likewise with her bequest more than a century later, in 1849.

John England died in 1724 and was briefly succeeded by his 26-year-old son, Revd John England junr, who died in 1735. The latter was the father of John England of Blandford whose son, Revd William England, defected to the Established Church and became rector of West Stafford and Archdeacon of Dorset.

The Sherborne Dissenters lost their evangelical voice when Revd William Prior left Dorset for London in 1738. His replacement, Revd William Cornish, stayed in place until his death in 1763. During his time, however, 'the zealots deserted' or, as they put it, 'rejected the Arian lie'. Cornish's espousal of this doctrine, dating from the fourth century, centred on the belief that 'the son of God was inferior to the creator'. Three-quarters of his flock denounced this as heresy and left the congregation in 1753. Alternative meetings were held in the private homes of William Russell, Benjamin Vowell, Samuel Vowell, Thomas Vowell and Benjamin Whitehead. Others voted with their feet, walking each Sunday to Milborne Port, where an independent meeting had been formed. They did not return until after the break-away movement had built 'a little bare chapel' beside the site that became Sherborne Brewery on the south side of Long Street. Revd Daniel Varder preached his first sermon there on 6 February 1757. The new community took to the Congregational cause but was 'small, poor, despised and persecuted' compared with the rump congregation of Presbyterians who retained their grip on well-endowed Newland Church.

Milborne Port, taking its name from a mill stream and an Anglo-Saxon place of commerce – not all ports were on the sea – was now becoming separated from Sherborne by a new landscape in which man took over from where the Creator left off. Cedars of Lebanon were the only exotic trees used by Lancelot 'Capability' Brown (1715–83) in his landscaping of Sherborne Park. The earliest British specimen of this Old World species is believed to be that beside Childrey Rectory in Oxfordshire. The setting of Raleigh's Seat and the view from the Hermit's Seat – before it was named Pope's Seat – were transformed by the building of the Cascade which makes for a

*Raleigh's Seat in the north-west corner of Sherborne Park, between his original Old Castle home and the replacement Sherborne Castle.*

dramatic departure point for the River Yeo from Sherborne Lake, over a stone waterfall and down to its ancient level below Dinney's Bridge. It is now supplemented by a modern outlet.

Sherborne Lake, covering 47 acres, was created in 1756. The idea is said to have come to Edward Digby, 6th Earl Digby, when he was so impressed with the temporary effect of a flash-flood that he decided to make it a permanent sheet of water. The rains had inundated Sir Walter Raleigh's ornamental gardens, terraces, water features, canals, lawns, bowling-green and orchard. They had also expanded the original large T-shaped pond – the former focal point – into a valley full of water.

The *Ginkgo biloba* growing beside Sherborne Castle has the distinction of being one of the first British specimens. A Palaeozoic tree, this is the oldest living fossil species in the world – unaltered for 200 million years, with delicate fleshy leaves and what is normally a multiple crown. The Sherborne tree, unfortunately, has lost its top. The species was introduced from China to Utrecht in 1730, to Kew Gardens in 1754, and to Sherborne before 1770.

The Industrial Revolution had also arrived in Sherborne. Historic Westbury Mill, beside the old course of the River Yeo east of the junction of Westbury and Ottery Lane (ST 637 159), was rented from Lord Digby by Spitalfields silk-maker John Sharrer in 1753. By 1755 he had a new 99-year lease which permitted him to pull down the buildings of the former grist-mill and to 'erect others in their stead for the better carrying on his business of silk throwing.' He spent £2,500 on rebuilding Westbury Mill and other premises in Sherborne which were leased from Benjamin Bastard. Sharrer's nephews George Ward of Sherborne and William Willmott (died 1787) of Hornsey were brought into the business in 1764.

The same year, Willmott took personal control, and expanded the enterprise with 'feeders' in Cerne Abbas and Stalbridge. In Cerne he rented the Isle Hall, above the Shambles in the Market Place, from Philip White. By 1768 there was another out station beside Law Way on the south side of the High Street in Bruton. Willmott also had 'a silk-house' in Dorchester and it was from the county town that he drew the money to pay an increasing wage bill across Dorset and Somerset. The town tended to run out of cash – causing Willmott to borrow gold, silver and copper coinage from Sherborne's attorneys, clergy and doctors – until Simon Pretor arrived from Lyme Regis in 1786. He established the Sherborne and Dorsetshire Bank, in his house in Long Street, in 1787. Pretor went into partnership with his three sons-in-law – Richard Pew, Samuel Whitty and Samuel Gill – and their descendants kept the tradition going, trading as an independent firm until being absorbed into the National Provincial Bank in 1850.

William Deering established a 'winding factory' in Bradford Abbas. The Paul and Vansomer families established a silk-throwing works on the Sherford stream, a tributary of the River Tone, in Upper High Street in Taunton. They borrowed an 'engine mistress' from Sherborne in order to teach the necessary skills. The business faltered, however, and William Willmott intervened with John Norman to buy the enterprise. Together they then established auxiliary winding-houses in Chard and Combe St Nicholas. Others followed in Ilchester and Tintinhull.

Here in Sherborne, a larger water-wheel was installed at Westbury Mill, over Whitsun in 1778, but the next problem was insufficient river flows. Half-production in dry months was maintained by a horse-walk powering the machinery during such times, after a horse mill had been built, in 1781. Even so, production remained seasonally intermittent, and it was not until November that Willmott could express relief that with 'water now plentiful' he 'shall work seven days a week'. He insured the business with the Sun Fire Office for £3,000.

Skeins of silk were wound on to bobbins, by engines, in a process which became Sherborne's main employer. From 1786 to 1826 there were '8,000 spindles at work and 600 hands' being employed by the Willmott family alone. Of these, 'some 250 windsters' were women and children. Many of them had previously been a burden on the poor rate. Weavers and silkmen, including disgruntled employees who set up in business on their own account, became the mainstay of the town's economy for the next two centuries.

Willmott faced fierce competition from William Cruttwell and Thomas Stidson in Sherborne, and from partners Fooks and Webb until he ended their 'long-contested opposition'. He bought their equipment and tools for £135 in November 1774. Cruttwell retired in February 1777 but was replaced by George Smout and his wife who set about converting Abbey Mill from corn to silk production. Despite these difficulties, which continued for a couple of decades, Westbury Silk Mill remained in the hands of Willmott's descendants until the twentieth century.

Silk came to Sherborne from all over the globe. Traditional sources such as Fossambrone, Reggio, Pesaro, Friuli and Bruttium in Italy, and Murcia in Spain, were augmented by bales from the silk roads into the Orient. The ancient provenances from Syria and Persia to Bengal and China were soon finding New World competition with imports from Pennsylvania. The price of these raw materials was £1.5s.0d. to £1.10s.0d. per pound and some consignments weighed in excess of 400 pounds.

The weather made the news from Sherborne on 20 January 1767:

*There has not been known here for thirty years past so deep a snow as last week. Our post which usually comes in about eight in the morning, did not arrive last*

*Monday till near ten at night. Our coaches have been stopped whole days and all our correspondence with distant parts greatly reduced. The frost still continues with severity and the snow lies on the ground. It is some satisfaction to find that in this extreme severity of weather when the pinchings of poverty must be felt even to torture by the poor, a spirit of benevolence prevails in a great number of places; and it is expected that the inhabitants of this town, who have always hitherto been almost the foremost in acts of benevolence, will open a subscription to alleviate the now indeed too grevious necessities of the poor.*

In the years after the Little Ice Age, English lakes provided sufficient ice for collection, removal and storage in brick-domed underground dungeons of which the ice-house in Sherborne Park is a rare example with its above-ground doors and housing still intact. It is a reminder of how cold our weather used to be. The nearby game larder is also a reminder of past priorities and pleasures. After providing exercise and sport in its collection, benevolent putrefaction improved, preserved and tenderised pheasant, partridge, wildfowl and venison to render them fit for marinating and the country-house table.

The orangery is a superb Robert Adam creation of c.1780. The luxury of a citrus spring was ensured whatever the severity of the winter. Another Adam building of this period is the boat-house, though it has since been supplemented by lesser structures elsewhere along the shoreline of the lake. The folly, in the north wall of Sherborne Park, between the two castles, was built as a ruined tower to act as an eye-catcher when seen from across the lake. The effect is currently lost as it is rendered inconspicuous by ivy. The same also applies to sections of the eighteenth-century castellated park wall. This garden feature replicated the medieval outer wall of the Old Castle but was set on the outside of its dry moat.

In February 1784, the weather in North Dorset was so severe that movements of raw and spun silk were disrupted between Cerne Abbas and Sherborne, and water-power for the 'twisting mill engine' ceased to flow. William Willmott appealed to his London customers for cash to alleviate the hardship. Among the donations 'to buy food for the starving children' was £10.10s.0d. from James Vere and Co. of Billingsgate.

Willmott's philanthropic endeavours included the Green Girls Society to encourage the advancement of female schooling. Education for girls in Sherborne had begun in a limited way in 1738 when the Blue Boys of Foster's School were joined by the first Green Girls. Teaching of the latter – though still subsidised by Foster's endowment – was then handed over to the first mistress of Lord Digby's School which was founded in 1743.

Opposite Raleigh's Seat, on the other side of the Cascade in Sherborne Park, stands the former Hermit's Seat which is now known as Pope's Seat.

It overlooks the Cascade and was renamed and rebuilt in honour of the poet Alexander Pope (1688–1744) who was a friend of William Digby, the 5th Baron Digby (1661–1752). The view from the Hermit's Seat, on Pope's 1724 visit, would have been across Raleigh's water gardens rather than Capability Brown's flood as we see it today. Sherborne Castle fascinated Pope who reflected in 1722 that it was 'so peculiar and in its position of so uncommon kind, that it merits a more particular description.'

Sherborne Abbey also has its Alexander Pope associations, literally carved in stone, on the graves of two of Digby's children. These poetical inscriptions are in memory of Robert Digby, the 5th Baron's second son, and Mary Digby, his eldest daughter.

The iron-railed grave of free-press pioneer Robert Goadby (1721–78) stood beneath a tall elm in the field south of Oborne Chapel (ST 653 177) until the bicentenary of his death. Then with a cruel twist of fate the tree was dead with Dutch elm disease and its fellers made such a mess of its removal that Goadby's memorial was completely smashed.

A further irony was that the destruction was completely ignored by the *Western Gazette* – the organ which Goadby had founded, via his *Western Flying Post* of 1743 – and it was left to the author to print the story, in 1978, in *Dorset County Magazine*. Goadby merged his paper with the *Sherborne Mercury* and had offices in Long Street, Sherborne. This was Sherborne Printing House and its ideals were inscribed above the door: 'The liberty of the Press, and the liberty of the People fall together. May heaven avert it.'

The Oborne grave, placed in the field between the chapel and the later railway line, was originally planted with a pine tree. It was a railed rectangle about ten feet by seven feet, and the stone was a celebration of the beauty of nature rather than the power of the printed word:

> *IN MEMORY OF MR ROBERT GOADBY LATE OF*
> *SHERBORNE, PRINTER, WHO DEPARTED THIS*
> *LIFE AUGUST 11TH 1778 AGE 57*
> *Death is a path that must be trod*
> *If man would ever come to God*
> *The fir tree aspires to the sky*
> *And is enclosed with everlasting verdure*
> *Emblem of the good and of that everlasting life*
> *Which God will bestow on them*
> *Since death is the gate to life*
> *The grave should be crowned with flowers.*
> *Here also lies Rachel, his wife*
> *Who died March 10th 1798.*

Revd William Sharpe (1724–83) was born in Houghton le Spring in the Durham coalfield. As vicar of Long Burton and Holnest, in the countryside south of Sherborne, he retained a vision of pit-heads and slag heaps which he was sure would come to this green and pleasant land. He arrived in 1763 and published his *Treatise upon Coal Mines* in 1769. The following year he documented previous prospecting failures with *An Appendix to a Treatise on Coal Mines*, containing an historial account of the several attempts formerly made to find coal in the environs of Sherborne, interspersed with remarks upon the imperfection and inefficacy of those attempts.

The favourite location for a dig was among the old marble quarries of Highmore's Hill, in the parish of Castleton, on the ridge east of Oborne. The main road passes into Somerset here at Crackmore Rocks. Above the road, on the south side, the hilltop (ST 666 181) is capped with a fossiliferous deposit of Forest Marble mixed with a blue clay almost indistinguishable from that found in true mining districts. That, and a fair amount of greed, was enough to trigger five attempts at sinking a mine shaft; around the years 1690, 1705, 1717, 1720 and 1740.

Another outcrop of the Forest Marble is on West Hill to the south of Sherborne, in Castleton parish, where the old turnpike road can be traced as a sunken trackway to the west of the present A352 main road, which dates from 1848 (ST 640 145). Here the diggers at least found something which might burn, but the smell was offensive; as Sharpe says 'a foul kind of coal was found and arrived at Sherborne and burnt upon the hearths.'

This area towards Leweston was also explored at Dykehead (ST 641 120) in about 1705 by Henry Thynne, son of the first Viscount Weymouth. Dr Hugh Torrens has shown that with all these attempts there was probably enough fossil wood found to keep the search alive by at least producing something that might just about burn.

There was a dig into different strata at Holnest Common (ST 650 090) in 1765 but the Oxford clay looks much like the Forest Marble. That too was a waste of time; coal in Dorset remained at 18d. a bushel compared with 4d. in the Somerset coalfield.

In October 1779, with fears of an invasion by the combined French and Spanish fleet massed off Plymouth, 1,000 French prisoners were marched out of the West Country, passing through Sherborne, on their way to Winchester. A more insidious threat to the town's economy was the disruption by war of the world's silk roads and enemy privateers harassing vessels importing bales that made it as far as the high seas. The Dorset Militia was quartered in Sherborne in March 1780. As Turkish silk failed to leave the Mediterranean there was additional hardship caused by the absence of the ships into Weymouth which used to carry back hogsheads of Cerne Abbas ale as a return consignment as far as the Thames.

This had become such a regular by-product of William Willmott's businesses that he continued to send barrels of beer to London by road. Willmott had been reluctant to give business to Sherborne carrier John Andrews – whom he regarded as dilatory – but he frequently hired the wagons of Edward Hatherell

and his daughter, Sarah, who continued the business after his death in 1777. Lilley's stagecoach took urgent messages, as it called in at Sherborne three days a week on the route from Taunton to London. Robert Oke was the principal carrier between Sherborne and Bristol. The two-way silk trade also brought luxuries to Sherborne, both in terms of fashionable clothes from London tailors Benedict Shield and John Boucher, and an occasional unlucky dip with tickets for the Irish lottery. There were high-class consumables such as those Willmott ordered for a christening party. This was for his son, Thomas, in January 1779. Owing to the fact that the conflict was interrupting supplies, alternatives were specified:

*Four quarts of real turtle soup from Horton's, by the Royal Exchange; if it cannot be had, then the same quantity of mock turtle. A fore-quarter of the best house lamb to be had. A turbot of 14 pounds or 15 pounds, or if not obtainable, then a fine cod fish.*

The Willmotts acquired 'almost daily' doses of medicine, from Drs Cumming and Johnson, and were inoculated by surgeon and apothecary Sampson Boys against smallpox in the epidemic of January 1782. John Mellier was the family's main medicine man from 1792 to 1794. Names changed according to the illness with Willmotts being prepared to try anyone and anything once they became desperate for a cure. They also relied upon Benjamin Vowell who was Sherborne's wine merchant.

Sherborne School came to terms in 1796 with upheavals in France and the concept of a new British Empire, by introducing history and geography into the curriculum, though learning French came at an additional charge. It was also relegated to sessions after regular hours where the 'language of diplomacy' was placed on a par with dancing lessons. Another optional extra that appears on accounts – one which many parents chose not to pay – was for a 'Single Bed'. In the time of headmaster John Cutler most of the boys 'were packed eight or ten in tiny dormitories'.

Cutler was a former naval chaplain who had been wounded in action on 6 July 1782, in the 74-gun battleship HMS *Hero* – 'a fine ship-of-the-line' – and had the background and kudos to attract the sons of titled and service families. They admired their headmaster and were treated to a relatively relaxed regime. During this period the school, or King's School as it was more formally known, evolved into one of England's 'great or public schools'. It produced a great legal mind in Samuel March Phillipps (1780–1862) from Moor Crichel, near Wimborne, whose 1814-published *Treatise on the Law of Evidence* became a standard textbook in Britain and America. Sir James Lewis Knight-Bruce (1791–1866), a judge, was one of the first two Lord Justices of Appeal appointed by Lord John Russell in his reforms of 1851.

# Sherborne Park

Left: *Boat-house on the western shore of Sherborne Lake, not quite up to the standards of Robert Adam, but characterful in its own right.*

Below: *The orangery is a Robert Adam building of c.1780.*

Below left: *Looking down on the Cascade (bottom left) and south-eastwards across Sherborne Lake to Sherborne Castle (top centre).*

Below: *Sherborne Park waterfall – known as the Cascade – in 1905.*

Above: *Turkish field gun, performing gate-guard duty, brought back from the Palestinian campaign in the First World War.*

Above: *Monk's Walk was graced by giant Virginia cedars* (centre) *after specimen trees were brought to Sherborne Park from the New World by Raleigh's traders.*

Left: *The game larder.*

Right: *Remarkable and fragile iron-grille ornamentation topping the entrance to the orangery garden.*

Below: *That Izaac Walton moment – 'the Contemplative Man's Recreation' – looking across Sherborne Lake to Sherborne Castle in 1994.*

Above: *A cottage ornée in the trees beside the foothills of Jerusalem.*

Right: *After the Little Ice Age, English lakes provided sufficient ice for collection and storage, with this eighteenth-century ice-house being a rare example of its kind, complete with above-ground doors and housing still intact.*

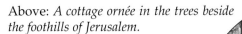

Above: *The Cascade and Pope's Seat – rebuilt on the poet's favourite spot – from the south in 1994.*

Above: *The stable block, seen from the south-east, typical of the most important building in English country-house life.*

Right: *Park wall, an eighteenth-century castellated garden feature, replaced the medieval outer wall of the Old Castle but on the outside of its dry moat.*

Centre right: *Friendly fallow deer fawn responding to a photo-call in Sherborne Park.*

Left: *Horse show in Sherborne Park, photographed by Colonel John Mennell, in 1973.*

Below: *The Manthorp Mudcat, here beginning to clear the reed-filled Sherborne Lake in 1973.*

Below left: *The Folly was built in the eighteenth century in the form of a ruined tower, as an eye-catcher when seen across the water from Sherborne Castle, but ivy has now rendered it inconspicuous.*

*Park Wall from the Old Castle, southwards across Sherborne Lake, to Sherborne Castle.*

*Fifteen*

# Nineteenth Century

The silk industry in Sherborne, having been continued after William Willmott's death by his widow, was taken over by their second son, Thomas, in December 1800. Expansion continued after the naval threat of the French Wars was removed by the Battle of Trafalgar. In 1809, following his father's example at Westbury Mill, Thomas Willmott bought another Sherborne corn-mill. This was East Mill, otherwise known as Castle Mill, at Castleton. The next acquisition, Oke's Mill or the Middle Mill, had already been converted to silk production. It was bought from competitor William Burnet in 1814.

William Noake, a 20-year-old Sherborne tanner, was convicted of burglary and sentenced to death in 1816. This was commuted, however, to transportation for seven years, to New South Wales, and he was taken from Dorchester Castle gaol to the *Laurel* hulk in Portsmouth Harbour on 20 May 1817.

George Rolls, a 19-year-old Sherborne labourer, was committed to Dorchester Castle on 1 October 1819 on a charge of housebreaking. He was sentenced to death but this was reprieved, for seven years' transportation, with his journey starting with the walk to the *Leviathan* hulk at Portsmouth on 28 June 1820.

Sherborne sawyer Elias Chippett – 27 years old and 'otherwise known as Sansom' – was taken to Dorchester Castle on 27 July 1821, having been accused of highway robbery. As was the custom he was sentenced to death but reprieved. His alternative, however, was transportation for life, leaving for the *York* hulk at Portsmouth on 5 November 1821.

Dr Ralph Lyon succeeded Revd John Cutler at Sherborne School in 1823. As well as its revived public-school status it was still 'a free grammar school for the boys of Sherborne and the country round' and would remain so until the Endowed Schools Act of 1871.

James Beazley junr, a 23-year-old Sherborne mason, appeared at the Lent Assize in Dorchester in March 1825 accused of stealing barley. He had a previous conviction, for which he was sentenced to four months' hard labour in 1823, for stealing hay, and another misdemeanour resulting in two weeks' imprisonment. His fate in 1825 was the forced march across Dorset and Hampshire to the *Leviathan* in Portsmouth followed by transportation to Australia. The period of his sentence was seven years but for most this effectively meant life.

Sherborne's pre-railway lifeline to the outside world, leaving from the Angel Inn, were coaches every other day, such as the Royal Clarence to the Bell and Crown Inn, Holborn, via an overnight stop in Salisbury. A cross-country service, also on alternate days, was the John Bull Coach which joined fashionable Bath spa with the seaside at Weymouth. The former Angel Inn, on the Green, carries the message 'Licensed to Let Post Horses' above its front door. 'C. Johnson' was the landlord's name above it in 1825, when its advertisement boasted: 'Good post horses with careful drivers. Superior Clarences and Broughams on hire. Neat wines, and foreign spirituous liquors. Hearse and mourning coaches.' Having been a busy coaching inn since 1750, the Angel Hotel and Commercial Inn became a boarding-house in 1865, as was bought for Sherborne School by Lord Iliffe in 1929.

King George IV died on 26 June 1830 and was succeeded by William IV. Anarchy and revolution were in the air and then literally in the winter sky, as barns, ricks and threshing-machines were torched and country houses threatened. Ten shillings was being demanded as a weekly living wage for agricultural labourers. Unrest coalesced into action on the ground as the Captain Swing riots spread westwards from Kent. The cognomen in which the threats were made came from the 'Babes in the Wood' from the Ingoldsby Legends by Sir Walter Scott: 'And Captain Swing came in the night,/And burnt all his beans and his barley.'

A letter was sent to Major Edward Castleman in Chettle House, near Sixpenny Handley, from 'The Handley Torches'. Edward Berkeley Portman of Bryanston House then marshalled a militia of '200 armed and mounted' plus '2,000 pedestrian special constables ready to resist any mob.' Many of his peers feared that these would not be sufficient. The panic-stricken gentry pleaded with the Home Secretary, Viscount Melbourne, to send in the regular Army.

Sir Colin Campbell, in general command of the district, was requested in December 1830 to send two troops of Lancers up through the troubled Blackmore Vale, from Blandford to Sturminster Newton, Stalbridge and Wincanton. C.B. Wollaston from Dorchester, visiting Moreton House, reported it was found it in a state of siege:

*I found Moreton barricaded like an Irish mansion – and arms provided for a few, but nothing has been wanted, though the barricade is continued. A spy was evidently employed the evening of Friday to see whether there was any preparation and it is most probable their report has prevented the attack.*

Two night-watchmen were employed to guard Sherborne School, at 1s.6d. each per night, for 22 nights that December. In 1831 the situation was inflamed by the hard-fought contest for the Dorset Parliamentary seat between privilege and the people. The former won through by a narrow margin with Lord Ashley, son and heir of the Earl of Shaftesbury of St Giles House, Wimborne St Giles, defeating William Ponsonby.

After disappointed radicals dispersed from the fairground hustings at Poundbury Camp, news of the result arrived in Sherborne, being announced from the Town Hall. Incensed at the gentry's successful resistance to Ponsonby and the cause of electoral reform, a group of flag-bearing militants set off down Newland towards Sherborne Castle, smashing windows as they went. They marched to the sound of pipe and drum. More glass was stoned on two sides of the Castle but estate hands drove them away. Returning to the town, they were halted by the newly appointed Revd John Parsons, who tried to quell the crowd by reading the Riot Act. Instead of dispersing, they took out their anger on the Vicarage, which was looted. Parsons wrote to a friend:

*They have entered and destroyed, and carried away much furniture and have broken every window and window-frame, before, and towards my garden. They have entered the cellar and having drank their fill left the barrels to empty themselves.*

On receiving news of the riot in Sherborne, James Frampton of Moreton House wrote to the Home Secretary, Lord Melbourne, asking for regular troops to be sent to secure the county. In the event, the following day, the Dorset Yeomanry rode into Sherborne. Acting as a local militia, with a commendable degree of moderation, they defused the situation by issuing musket balls. The only casualties were yeomen hit by stones, or hurt when a horse slipped and fell on cobblestones, and after the arrival of regular troops in the evening there was no more visible unrest on the streets. Nine men were charged in connection with the Sherborne riot. Of these, six were acquitted, but the three who led the procession with para-military props – flag, drum and pipe – were convicted. Each was sentenced to two years' hard labour. John Perry, editor of the *Sherborne Mercury*, was forced to resign from the Dorset Yeomanry after criticism for having failed to turn out during the incident.

A Royal Commission was appointed in 1832 to look into rural poverty and its recommendations were incorporated into the Poor Law Act of 1834. The Poor Law Institution of Sherborne Union, popularly (or unpopularly) known as the Workhouse, was a stone-built block besides Horsecastles. Built in 1837, it housed 240 inmates from both the town and surrounding parishes.

Gas lighting was introduced in Sherborne in 1839 with the first fittings in Sherborne School being installed in 1840. Sherborne Gas Works stood beside the railway line on the west side of Gas House Hill where the manager's house survives and has an 1836 date stone.

Westbury Mill expanded from its original site in 1840, into the tall purpose-built sheds of a new Sherborne Silk Mill on the other side of the Westbury junction, along the east side of Factory Lane (which is now known as Ottery Lane, from a family of that name rather than associations with otters). Its low-set windows let in light at hand-working height. Workers were accommodated in a great Ham stone terrace, south-facing towards the works from the north side of Horsecastles, of which 36 dwellings survive. Robert Willmott (1814–75) ran the business after his father, John Percival Willmott (1804–58), moved into Sherborne House in Newland.

The hymn-writer John Mason Neale (1818–66), an old Shirburnian, turned his childhood memory of snow lying across the Courts into the memorable 'deep and crisp and even' line of his carol celebrating Good King Wenceslas.

An era ended with the death of William Hyde (1751–1845) who had been organist at Sherborne Abbey since 1776, a period of 69 years, which must have been a record for there or anywhere. He was also responsible for expanding the choir, from ten to a dozen 'boys of this town' as a 'Choir of Singers' subject to training sessions twice a week as well as regular attendance at 'Divine Service'. By 1823, however, there was friction between the choir and reformist vicar Revd John Parsons – catalyst for the Sherborne riot – who insisted upon 'congregational singing'. It was a battle that Hyde and his boys were to win, by 64 votes to 15 at a parish meeting, following which Parsons had to swallow his pride as the organist and choir resumed their traditional roles.

Dorset's links with the Digby family moved sideways with the death of Edward Digby, 8th Baron Digby and 2nd Earl Digby (1773–1856). He died unmarried, which resulted in the extinction of the earldom, but the English barony of Digby and its Irish counterpart passed to a first cousin, Edward St Vincent. The eldest son of Admiral Sir Henry Digby, he became the 9th Earl Digby and moved into Minterne House, Minterne Magna.

Edward Digby bequeathed Sherborne Castle and its estate to his sister, Charlotte, who married William Wingfield. This branch of the family and their descendants took the name Wingfield-Digby.

Inventor and old Shirburnian William Ellis Metford (1824–99), who left Sherborne in 1841, was 'one of the earliest experimenters in double rocket propulsion.' From 1846 to 1850 he was a construction engineer for the Wiltshire, Somerset and Weymouth Railway which passes west of Sherborne, via Pen Mill, and became Yeovil Junction in 1860. The son of a doctor, Metford had a rifle-range behind his home at Flook House, Taunton, where he invented the exploding bullet in 1857. This was adopted in 1863. He also invented the breech-loading rifle, in 1870, and provided the weapon with which Sir Henry St John Halford won a principal prize at the Wimbledon military shooting competition in 1871. The Metford bore was combined with a bolt action, by the American James P. Lee, for the Lee-Metford service rifle in 1888. Metford, who had moved to Redland, Bristol, bequeathed a pair of library globes to Sherborne School.

From 1845 until 1850, when he retired through illness, Revd Charles Thomas Penrose was headmaster of the school. A real-life character from *Tom Brown's Schooldays*, he had failed in his attempt at stepping into the shoes of his former headmaster, Dr Thomas Arnold, at Rugby. Instead, he brought rugby football to Sherborne, starting the great tradition in 1846, though at the time most of his contemporaries agreed with Samuel Butler that this was a game 'fit only for butchers'.

Penrose came to Sherborne as a 29-year-old ex-Trinity rowing blue who had competed against Leander and Oxford. By the end of the decade, as Penrose fought debilitating illness, the school roll had declined catastrophically, to just two boarders and 38 day-boys from the town. Its revival – 'to the cusp of 300' – took place under the management of Hugo Daniel Harper. The founder of the Headmasters' Conference, he was an advocate of positive thinking, and brought a personal motto to match: 'Give me a man with Go!'

Sherborne Congregational stalwart Benjamin Chandler, who was also chairman of the Local Board of Health, challenged the statutes of Sherborne School in 1851. He claimed they maintained unfair provisions from the time when 'Popery was but beginning to lose its hold on the nation' which had become 'inexpedient and unjust'. He pointed out that Dissenters 'presently number perhaps 50 per cent of the church-going population of this town' and took his case to the Court of Chancery in 1852, petitioning against:

*1 The compulsory use of prayers in the School, which are specified in the ordinances, and which imply or assert doctrines disapproved of more or less by various classes of Dissenters.*
*2 The compulsory attendance of scholars at Church.*
*3 The religious instruction which all the scholars are compelled to receive, which includes learning the Catechism of the Church of England and other doctrines of the Church.*
*4 The fact that exhibitions and pecuniary rewards and distinctions are to be conferred exclusively on persons going to the Universities of Oxford and Cambridge.*

The last provision, about the Oxbridge universities,

was offensive to Congregationalists because entry into them was effectively barred to Dissenters. Sir John Romilly, the Master of the Rolls, referred to a judgment by Lord Macclesfield and agreed there was a *prima-facie* case for saying that such rules were 'more exclusive than required'. He decided, however, that he had no jurisdiction over the matter, as it should have been taken in the first instance to the Lord Chancellor.

Benjamin Chandler did just that, petitioning Lord Cranworth 'to recover for the children of Dissenters their ancient privileges in matters of religion.' He asked the governors of Sherborne School to voluntarily add a clause dispensing with Church attendance and the learning of the Catechism by 'the children of persons conscientiously dissenting from the doctrine or discipline of the Church of England.'

The governors resisted until they received a subpoena which returned the matter – now with a legitimate remit – to the Court of Chancery. Here Lord Chancellor Cranworth followed Romilly's lead, citing the Macclesfield judgement of 1723, and found against them in a case which cost the school £500. Reinforced by new statutes in 1854, this became an interdenominational restoration of liberties, applicable nationwide, as King Edward VI had also granted similar charters to other grammar schools. Oxford and Cambridge also reconsidered their position and eventually repealed their religious requirements in 1871.

Some 20 Shirburnians went to war in the Crimea in 1854 and 24 served in the Indian Mutiny in 1857. Rear-Admiral Henry James Raby, VC (1827–1907), who entered the Royal Navy in 1842, returned to London from the subcontinent and had the distinction of being the first to receive the Victoria Cross for valour in person from the Queen. He commanded a squadron of boats in the capture and destruction on Porto Novo and on coming back from West Africa was put in charge of HMS *Adventure* to sail for China from 1868–71. As a pensioner he lived in Clarence Parade, Southsea.

Boy-soldier Charles George Palmer (1847–1940) was unique for a Shirburnian in being awarded his combat medal and clasp – for the 'Defence of Lucknow' – before he arrived at Sherborne School. Nine years old, he volunteered for battery duties with the gunners during the most bitterly fought siege of the Indian Mutiny, and ran with messages through the carnage. Then his 19-year-old sister was killed in front of him by a cannon-ball. The son of General Henry Palmer of the India Staff Corps, he was sent to England and Sherborne in 1858, but insisted upon returning to India in 1863 and became an irrigation engineer. He retired to Quamichan Lake, Duncan, on Vancouver Island and was the last holder of the Lucknow medal when he died in British Columbia, aged 93, during the Second World War.

Leading character actor William Macready (1793–1873), Dickens' closest friend, toured the

United States and became embroiled in a tiff with his critics, during which he was called a 'superannuated driveller', and appeared as Macbeth to New York's Broadway on 10 May 1849 to the worst recorded riot in theatrical history. Some 17 people were shot dead when troops opened fire.

Macready returned to England and in 1851 'withdrew' to his home in Sherborne. This was the impressive classical three-storey Sherborne House, built about 1720, on the north side of Newland. Lord Digby's School for Girls moved into it in 1931.

'Mac', as he was known to Charles Dickens (1812–70) prevailed upon the famous author to come down to read his novel *A Christmas Carol* at a literary institute 'in the busy town of Sherborne, in Dorsetshire'. The novelist, his wife and sister-in-law stayed a couple of days, until 23 December 1854, and then went home for Christmas.

Dickens had written *The Lamplighter*, a play, for Macready in 1838, for a performance at the Covent Garden Theatre. It was never acted, and in 1841 Dickens rewrote it as 'The Lamplighter's Story' in *The Pic Nic Papers* and donated the proceeds to a trust fund for the widow and children of publisher John Macrone, who had died in poverty.

The novelist named his second daughter, Kate Macready Dickens, for the actor, in October 1839. That month Macready attended the dinner in celebration of the completion of *Nicholas Nickleby*, at the Albion, Aldersgate Street, near the Barbican. 'You must come and see my house when we have it to rights,' Dickens wrote to Macready in November 1839. That was No. 1 Devonshire Terrace, Regents Park, which the author would occupy until 1851.

Macready and the Irish revolutionary Daniel O'Connell were among those distressed in 1840 by the killing-off of Little Nell in *The Old Curiosity Shop*. Not that the tragic ending was the author's idea; it had been suggested to him by biographer John Forster.

Dickens cited Mac's company as a reason for staying home in July 1841. 'The moral of all this is that there is no place like home,' he wrote to Forster, on being told he had been invited to a dinner in his honour in Glasgow. 'I sigh for Devonshire Terrace and Broadstairs, for battledore and shuttlecock; I want to dine in a blouse with you and Mac.'

The Macreadys looked after the four children when Mr and Mrs Dickens visited America in 1842. Disappointed with what they found, Dickens told Macready that the republic was not that of his imagination, being defective even in comparison with England, 'bad and faulty as the old land is'. As for 'freedom of opinion', it did not exist, and he had been advised not to put his views of America on paper because the Americans could not bear to hear of their faults. They were, however, acceptable as individuals, and the scenery was immense to an extent beyond description, as with the endless solitude of the prairies.

In June 1843 Dickens was at the head of the table for a dinner at the Star and Garter, Richmond, in honour of Macready, when the actor retired from the Drury Lane Theatre and was about to set off on his first tour of America. Dickens was the life and soul of a birthday party for one of Macready's children, dancing – in the novelist's words – like 'a country gentleman of independent property, residing on a tip-top farm, with the wind blowing straight in my face every day.' He and John Forster performed conjuring tricks, producing a plum pudding 'from an empty saucepan, held over a blazing fire kindled in Stanfield's hat without damage to the lining' and changing a box of bran 'into a live guinea-pig' to the 'unspeakable admiration of the whole assembly'.

When they were not together they kept up a constant correspondence. 'Between *Copperfield* and *Household Words*, I am as busy as a bee,' Dickens wrote to Mac on returning from Brighton in June 1850. 'May the former be as good a book as I hope it will be for your children's children to read.'

Dickens organised the staging of Macready's last public performance at Drury Lane, and a public dinner, on 1 March 1851, that was presided over by Sir Edward Bulwer Lytton.

The novelist told Macready that he was tempted on laying down his 'book-pen' to 'run out on the breezy downs here, tear up the hills, slide down the same, and conduct myself in a frenzied manner, for the relief that only exercise gives me.'

He was also using his pen politically, pointing out to Lord Lyttelton on 16 August 1855 that although Macready, as an actor-manager, had faced opposition for 'rigorously weeding out that great indecency' of prostitution in the theatre, he persisted in this throughout the time of his management. Subsequently, Webster had managed to cleanse the Haymarket and rescue 'the saloon and passages from the defilement, and made the house quite reproachless in that particular.'

Similarly with the Adelphi, but Dickens went on to note that the problem had transferred itself to 'a certain dancing establishment... (I mean a Ball Room) which great numbers of women regularly frequent.' The police were showing 'a sound discretion in not interfering with it' and although it was noted to have the effect of draining off the 'stragglers' who might otherwise have frequented the theatres with lax managers, Dickens took a pragmatic view: 'It is always to be borne in mind that, in a great city, prostitution will be somewhere.'

In 1856, on describing the civil service as the 'Circumlocution Office' Dickens wrote to Mac that it had been necessary to let off 'a little indignant steam which would otherwise blow me up.'

Later in the year that 'book-pen' was in full flow:

*Calm amidst the wreck, your aged friend glides away on the Dorrit steam, forgetting the uproar for a stretch of hours, refreshing himself with a ten or twelve miles' walk, pitches headforemost into foaming rehearsals, placidly emerging for editorial purposes, smokes over buckets of distemper with Mr Stansfield aforesaid, again calmly floats upon the Dorrit waters.*

Macready remarried in 1860 and moved to Cheltenham. Dickens continued to write. On 18 October 1869 he described to Mac his 'preliminary agonies of a new book' which turned out to be *The Mystery of Edwin Drood*. Dickens died before it was finished.

The actor followed in 1873 and is buried at Kensal Green. He was said to have led his life in a manner that was often indistinguishable from his acting persona, being at best introspective, and frequently 'unamiable and almost morose as well as violent'. Both on stage and off his behaviour was marked by instant changes from one extreme to the other, from curses to courtesies, and he could physically work himself into a frenzy for a performance.

Louis Ruegg (1822–1905) bought the *Sherborne Journal* and its printing offices in South Street in 1858. He had been associated with the newspaper since 1843 and claimed 'to beat even *The Times* in our delivery of intelligence.' Ironically, the approach of the railroad was destined to help the national press more than its local competition, though at the time Ruegg believed the reverse would be the case. The Salisbury and Yeovil Railway, which Ruegg encouraged other residents to back, saw rising share prices and gave healthy dividends as it neared its target and planned the next move onwards to Exeter. What is now the Waterloo to Exeter alternative to the West of England main line – from Paddington – opened to passenger traffic in four stages:

*Salisbury to Gillingham – 2 May 1859.*
*Gillingham to Sherborne – 7 May 1860.*
*Sherborne to Hendford, Yeovil – June 1860.*
*Bradford Abbas Junction to Exeter – 19 July 1860*
    *(leaving the Yeovil Town line as a cul-de-sac branch from Yeovil Junction Station).*

The first sod was cut in the spring of 1856, at Gillingham, where Ruegg joined the directors in toasting the success of the line as the heavens opened. One of the promoters observed: 'We've had so much cold water thrown upon us before this that a bucket or two extra can make no difference now.'

What they called the Central Line, between Castleman's Corkscrew to the Dorset coast and Isambard Kingdom Brunel's wide-guage line to Bristol, faced a barrage of obstructions triggered by national and international events. Henry Ker-Seymer, MP, from Hanford House, joked at the opening banquet of the insuperable odds they had overcome:

*We proved the case but we never got the line. We were*

*unfortunate. Whenever we had a chance there was sure to be another commercial or diplomatic crisis.*
*The Central Line – war on the Indian Frontier!*
*The Central Line – Potato Famine in Ireland!*
*The Central Line – Money at 7 to 8 percent!*
*The Central Line – France has another Revolution!*
*The Central Line – Another deficient harvest!*
*The Central Line – War between Russia and Turkey!*
*The Central Line – Wheat at £20 a load!*

The problem in the background, until financiers and traders subverted the wider countryside with proof that greed could deliver yields, was the resistance of Dorset's powerful landowners who had already spiked so many earlier railway projects on what seemed to be logical lines across the map.

George Townsend told a meeting in Sherborne on 26 March 1846 that it was time to challenge the primacy of the Great Western Railway. Townsend called it the 'Great Way Round company'. Both Robert Gordon of Leweston, a former Secretary to the Treasury, and Lord Digby had thrown their 'territorial influence in the same direction'. Set against them were the silk-factory owners of Sherborne and the glovers of Milborne Port who crowded the Town Hall in Sherborne and declared that 'a drop line from Sparkford' was no alternative to a direct line to London.

The Yeovil line was soon to be subject to similar derision given that it 'came no nearer to Yeovil than Sutton Bingham'. Coming too close to places was also a problem and the 'residential injury' to the Wingfield-Digby family at Sherborne Castle and the Medlycotts of Ven House, Milborne Port, was mitigated by a promise that the 'direct route' would not pass within sight of their homes.

The London and South Western Railway, which opened as the Salisbury and Yeovil Railway, started with cannon-fire when the first train ran down the line on 7 May 1860. It brought Sherborne to within four and a half hours of the capital terminus at Waterloo. These days the times are halved with the post-privatisation operators, South West Trains, being a subsidiary of Stagecoach Plc. The former Digby Hotel in Digby Road – now accommodation for Sherborne School – was rebuilt 'contemporaneously with the construction of the railway', to quote novelist Thomas Hardy. He features it, as the Earl of Wessex Hotel in Sherton Abbas, in *The Woodlanders*.

Westwards from Sherborne, towards Yeovil Junction, the line took a straight and determined course through the hamlet of Wyke (ST 601 145) in the outlying extremity of Castleton parish. Here it literally separated the moated house from its farmyard and historic barn at the end of a cul-de-sac lane east of Bradford Abbas.

The Digby Mausoleum in the back part of the town cemetery, off Lenthay Road (ST 630 160), was built at a cost of £38,000 in 1862. It is highly ornate, in mock-Byzantine style, and was built over a crypt by architect William Slater for the Wingfield-Digby family. The marble floor can be lowered by hydraulic lift. The outer door is set in an immense flourish of heavy carving.

The *Sherborne Journal*, evoking memories of Robert Goadby, celebrated its centenary in 1864 and proprietor Louis Ruegg found himself the subject of a presentation from the subscribers. He received 'a purse containing 234 sovereigns, a handsome solid silver inkstand, and a beautifully engrossed vellum, containing the list of the donors.'

Ruegg, who had done so much to smooth the passage of the railway against sentimental and topographical resistance, then faced two decisive battles. In standing out against an initial tempting offer from the London and South Western Railway to reach a settlement, he ensured a better deal for himself and other shareholders in December 1872. His newspaper went in the other direction, joining the *Western Flying Post* of old, in a merger that saw it absorbed into the *Western Gazette*. Louis Ruegg retained a lifelong interest in railways and their accountancy, being the auditor of the Waterloo and City Railway – known as 'the Drain' – and the Somerset and Dorset Railway across the western hills and vales.

Fire nearly destroyed one of Sherborne's historic taverns in January 1867. John Vincent's Mermaid Inn was then in South Street, before relocation to the top end of Blackberry Lane, where it faces the Bristol Road. The brewhouse, cellar, storeroom and the entire stock of beer and barrels were lost in the blaze, after midnight on a Friday night:

*The fire was discovered by Police Constable Freeman, who instantly called the inmates who were all in bed, and also gave an alarm. The engines were soon on the spot and did good service in containing the fire to the part of the building in which it originated.*

The Yeatman Hospital, in Hospital Lane, was built in 1866 as a memorial to Harry Farr Yeatman of Stock House at Stock Gaylard in the heart of the Blackmore Vale. Extra wings were added in 1914, 1927 and 1930. It remains the mainstay of local health facilities. A less practical memorial, between the south transept of Sherborne Abbey and Half Moon Street, is an elaborate Eleanor Cross – in imitation of those leading from Charing Cross to Waltham Abbey – which was erected on octagonal steps in 1884 on the site of the old Town Hall. It commemorates the life of George Digby Wingfield-Digby who died on 7 May 1883.

Castleton Water Works (ST 646 169), beside the meadow between Oborne Road and the railway, produced the town's first general supply of pure water. The 1868-built classically designed pump-house contains a 26-feet diameter cast-iron overshoot water-wheel which powered three vertical ram pumps. It is now operated by Wessex Water but the wheel has become a specimen of industrial archaeology.

The guardians of the chapel at Sherborne School in the 1860s and 1870s were its ravens. Moloch, who seems to have been the offspring of Jack and Grip from Raven's Nook, was 'a wretched ingrate' who swooped on the chapel steps and had a particular aversion 'to boys, hymn books and the headmaster's dog'.

The Conduit in Cheap Street, owned by Sherborne School, had been used as a public reading room until 1847, and was then the constabulary rest-room. By 1861 it was briefly used by the vicar, who attempted to run a penny-bank for the poor, and then had a humanitarian role during the Franco-Prussian War. Hospital supplies, produced by Sherborne schoolboys, included quantities of bedding: 'Fellows are constantly tearing up waste paper into minute pieces, for stuffing pillows, many of which have already been sent away.'

The Conduit was condemned as being 'in a very dilapidated condition' in 1872 and was also said to be 'an obstacle to traffic'. As a result the school governors agreed that it should be rebuilt. In doing so, all the pieces were stacked on the pavement, and it was then decided 'to kill two birds with one stone' by re-erecting it on that spot. In doing so, the building was removed from the carriageway, in work that revealed paving from the Abbey Lady Chapel. This had been reused, in repairs to the Conduit, after the Headmaster's House was built on the chapel site in 1560.

Foster's School tidied up its endowment fund in 1872 with an amalgamation of its historic charities. The names behind a dozen bequests, in chronological order, stretched across three centuries – Sir Thomas Horsey (1589), David Llewellen (1605), Agnes Foster (as Mrs Boughton, 1629), Richard Foster (1640), William Knoyle (1678), Dorothy Eastment (1686), George Connington (1698), Simon Whetcombe (c.1700), John Woodman (1717), Robert Avoke (1720), Robert Goadby (1778) and Charles Bull Hart (1805). The income allowed the school to increase its roll from 25 boys to 40 in 1881, with the institution being at that time 'in a more prosperous position than it had been for some time.'

New classrooms were built beside Hound Street in 1875. The aim of the reform, however, had also been to introduce higher education for girls in Sherborne. In the event, efforts were diverted into a new boarding-house for 30 boys, which was built by contractor George Pitman of Milborne Port in 1886. The *Sherborne Journal* announced its completion, at a cost of £1,248, on 18 February 1887:

*A master's new residence and boarding house in connection with the school has been built adjoining the old school block and connected therewith by a vestibule leading to the dining hall which had been converted out of one of the classrooms. The school now forms a commanding and conspicuous block of buildings, situated in a healthy and elevated part of the town overlooking the Slopes and Sherborne Park, with views extending into Somersetshire. The sanitary arrangements have been carried out in accordance with the latest known principles of sanitary science.*

All it now needed were the boys. These remained in short supply as a result of the Great Depression in English agriculture resulting from a collapse in prices caused by the advent of refrigeration and steamship imports from the New World. The Charity Commissioners remained displeased that girls received no benefit from what had been non-discriminatory mixed-sex bequests. They therefore proposed the transfer of part of the funds to Milton Abbas Girls' School which was based in Blandford. This infuriated the *Sherborne Journal*: 'Foster leaves money to found a school in his own town of Sherborne; Government officials appropriate this to a town 20 miles off!'

The commissioners backed down. An unholy coalition of clergy and closed-minded councillors continued to hold up proper provision for educating the girls of Sherborne for another decade. The town showed more interest in providing a prestige replacement for the Town Hall, beside the Market Place, which was demolished in 1884.

Fighting in the Afghan War, old Shirburnian Colonel Sir Arthur George Hammond, VC (1843–1919), won his Victoria Cross in 1879, and followed it with the Distinguished Service Order from the Hazara expedition of 1888. He was appointed aide-de-camp to Queen Victoria in 1890 and returned to Asia for the Isazai expedition of 1892, the Chitral relief force of 1895, and the Tirah expedition of 1897–98. He retired to Surrey's Army country at Camberley.

Canon Edward Malet Young took over from Dan Harper as headmaster of Sherborne School in 1877. Various unfortunate incidents were compounded by his adoption of the Liberal cause, chairing a public meeting, which 'fell foul of many of the Tory governors'.

A Dorset and Somerset literary dynasty were represented at Sherborne by 'Powys major' and 'Powys minor'. The first was author John Cowper Powys (1872–1963) who left to recover in Montacute Vicarage from dyspeptic stomach problems in the spring of 1891. The second, a future headmaster of Sherborne Preparatory School, was his brother Littleton Powys (1874–1955). It was a time when top-hats were compulsory on Sundays and to have been seen with a butterfly-net would have guaranteed a swishing. Littleton had to wait until he was 'well out of the town' before he unfolded his net.

School house tutor E.C. Malon almost came to blows with Canon Young in 1888, as a result of which he was dismissed, and sued the headmaster for defamation. Young was succeeded as headmaster by Revd Frederick Brook Westcott in January 1892. Jack Painter was the school's cricket coach, for the games Powys minor remembered from the hot summer of 1893, after which he joined brother John in

Cambridge. He was going through his Christian Socialist stage and being obtusely intellectual: 'You never think, Littleton. Why don't you think? You never think.'

Those with a military bent could join the 'Redcoats' of Sherborne School Cadet Corps which was formed as a cadet company of the Dorsetshire Regiment in 1888. One of the first intake, Sergeant Vernon Lewis, joined the Royal Scots Fusiliers and fought at Chitral in 1895, in the Niger operations of 1897 and 1898, and sailed to South Africa the following year. There he was killed during the Boer War, at Pieter's Hill, in 1900.

The first 'March Out' of the cadets took place on 11 December 1888 – before they were issued with rifles – and was an assault on imaginary defenders holding the Slopes and Terrace along to Dancing Hill to the south of the town:

*The Company, leaving Sherborne as the advanced guard of a Battalion, were ordered to clear Dancing Hill of the skirmishers of a phantom enemy; this they managed to do and successfully occupied the whole of the West Slopes and the Town Cricket Ground; after this bloodless victory they returned to Sherborne.*

The Corps received its first batch of 15 Martini Henry short-butt rifles, with bayonets, on 8 February 1889. These were followed by 70 unserviceable Snider carbines for drill purposes. There were also a pair of drums and some bugles. The new school song, by James Rhoades to music by Louis Napoleon Parker, celebrated their arrival: 'See where the Sherborne Redcoats come, with shrill of fife and tuck of drum.'

They paraded on the ice of Sherborne Lake in the big freezes of 1890 and 1895. The Freemasons' Hall – the Lodge of Benevolence – was being built on the north side of the present Police Station, in Digby Road. It is a small but confident piece of Victorian Ham stone architecture with an assertive façade, dated 1896, that became semi-secreted from the street by a mature cordon of ornamental trees.

Sherborne School for Girls was founded in 1899 through the generosity of John Kenelm Wingfield-Digby, MP (1859–1904), and his second wife, the former Miss Charlotte Digby from Galway.

The century closed with the fiercest of Empire conflicts. Britain's notable non-combatant contributor to the outcome of the South African War was Sir Godfrey Yeatman Lagden (1851–1934). This splendid old Shirburnian knew Africa as well as any Briton, having walked the Atlantic seaboard from the Cape to Ashanti on the Gold Coast, on a game-hunting trek in 1883 which bagged a unique wildlife collection. His diplomatic adroitness and understanding of black sensibilities were put to the test as Resident Commissioner of Basutoland on the outbreak of the conflict. He successfully thwarted Boer enlistment of 25,000 tribesmen.

# Sherborne School

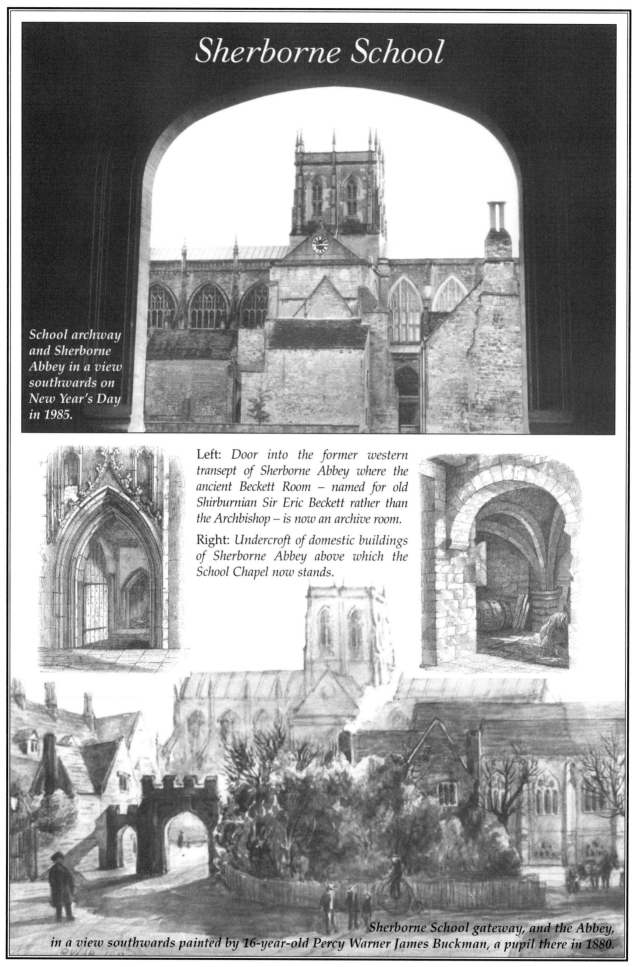

School archway and Sherborne Abbey in a view southwards on New Year's Day in 1985.

Left: *Door into the former western transept of Sherborne Abbey where the ancient Beckett Room – named for old Shirburnian Sir Eric Beckett rather than the Archbishop – is now an archive room.*

Right: *Undercroft of domestic buildings of Sherborne Abbey above which the School Chapel now stands.*

*Sherborne School gateway, and the Abbey, in a view southwards painted by 16-year-old Percy Warner James Buckman, a pupil there in 1880.*

*The scholastic and ecclesiastical town, northwards from the Abbey, across the roofs of the chapel of Sherborne School (left) and its Courts (centre) to the town's Methodist Church (right centre).*

Right: *North-westwards from the Abbey tower, over the Chapel of Sherborne School (centre) and its classrooms and laboratories to Acreman Street (middle distance).*

Below right: *The Courts in 1930, from the Abbey tower, after the completion of Sir Reginald Blomfield's extensions to Sherborne School.*

Above: *The corner of the English block southwards from the Abbey Road to the Almshouse.*

*The steps up from Abbey Road into 'BSR', which stands for the Big School Room.*

Above: *South-eastwards from the inner courtyard of Sherborne School to the Abbey clock at five minutes to three on New Year's Day in 1985.*

Below right: *School House, at the heart of Sherborne School, looking south-eastwards from the Courts.*

Above: *Gateway block and the tower, centrepiece for the entrance to the Courts (seen from there, looking north-east), was designed by Sir Reginald Blomfield in 1917 and built in 1923.*

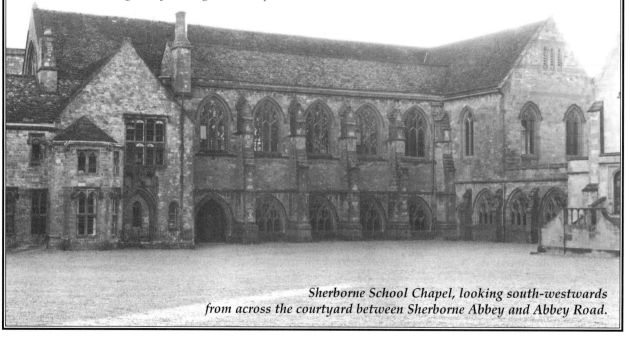

*Sherborne School Chapel, looking south-westwards from across the courtyard between Sherborne Abbey and Abbey Road.*

Above: *Sherborne School (centre) from the air in 1922 – before the building of the tower and Medlycott block – with other prominent buildings in this view from the west being Abbey House, the Methodist Church* (towards top left) *and Sherborne Abbey* (centre right).

Below: *Eastern door into the English block of Sherborne School, at the back of Sherborne Abbey and its stained-glass windows, in a view from the north in 1985.*

Above: *Sherborne School's coat of arms on the Tower* (left), *looking southwards from the junction of Hospital Lane and Abbey Road, with Sherborne Abbey peeking over the roof of gateway block.*

Right: *Three-storey School House, seen from the courtyard, converted into a single boarding-house in 1868, was rebuilt to match the rest of Sherborne School in 1887.*

*Early-nineteenth-century print of Old School and the Master's House, at a time when Sherborne School was known as the King's School.*

Left: *Looking down on the scene in the Courts as the Blackmore Vale Hunt gathers for a meet in the 1970s.*

Below: *Sherborne School Chapel (left), looking westwards from gateway block of the Courts.*

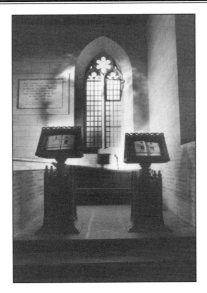

Above left: *Shadows of 'dark cowled Benedictines haunt the pillared shade' of the Cloisters, to quote James Rhoades who wrote the school song.*

Above centre: *Registers of remembrance in the antechamber of Sherborne School Chapel which was extended in 1920 'in loving memory of those Shirburnians who laid down their lives in the Great War.'*

Above right: *Blackmore Vale Hounds streaming out of Tower entrance, northwards into Abbey Road, in 1975.*

Right: *Doors of the former woodwork and metalwork rooms, in the time of teachers Annett and Crouch, since handed over to the arts department and refurbished as the Oliver Holt Gallery.*

Below: *Early-nineteenth-century neo-classical front of Abbey House* (centre), *acquired by Sherborne School in 1835, looking east along Abbey Road towards its porch columns* (behind boy) *and Cheap Street* (right).

This image: *Mid-Victorian print of Abbey House at Sherborne School.*

Below right: *Sherborne School as it was until 1860 with Bell Buildings (far left), Box Buildings dating from 1697 (centre and right), looking south-westwards from Abbey Road which then passed through the Courts.*

*Sexton's Cottage and former Silk Mill north-west of the Abbey, in 1850, before being taken over by Sherborne School.*

*A meet of the Blackmore Vale Hunt in the Courts of Sherborne School in about 1972.*

## Sixteen

# 1900–1909

The death bell at Sherborne Abbey still tolled for almost the entire daylight hours, once a year, on the Earl of Bristol's memorial day. Death bells were the sound of the new century. Capturing the military mood following the Boer War, Sherborne School Cadet Corps featured in the first movie film to be shot in the town, which was screened in a marquee at Pack Monday Fair in 1902. They then discarded their redcoats, adopting khaki uniforms in 1903, and began a process of extending membership to virtually the entire school by the end of the decade.

Sherborne School for Girls moved into its smart new brick and stone buildings, in Bradford Road, in 1903. The opening ceremony was performed by Charles Stewart Vane-Tempest-Stewart, 6th Marquess of Londonderry (1852–1915), former Viceroy of Ireland, who was president of the Board of Education and Lord-President of the Council.

Dramatist and composer Louis Napoleon Parker (1852–1944) was appointed director of music at Sherborne School in 1873. The only son of Charles Albert Parker, he had been born in Calvados, France. In Sherborne he married local girl Georgiana Calder, in 1878, and remained in post for 19 years. What he

is remembered for, however, was his return to the town in 1905 for the 'Mother of all Pageants' which used the ivy-clad ruins of the Old Castle as its main setting. Revd F.B. Westcott, headmaster of Sherborne School, starred as Bishop Aldhelm.

Parker made his reputation with the Sherborne event and was commissioned to do much the same for Warwick, Bury St Edmunds, Colchester, York and Dover. Performances continued during the First World War with the Pageant of Fair Women and the Pageant of Freedom. He was still active as an octogenarian, with the Kenilworth Pageant in 1939, until the next war intervened.

The Church Hall in Digby Road has a weathered stone bust incorporated into its façade. The subject was Mark Parsons, a butcher in Cheap Street, who was chief marshal of the pageant from which Pageant Gardens takes its name. Parsons, it was said, was of monumental build but it is rare to find a thin butcher. The Church Hall, as it is known, was built as the Digby Memorial Hall in 1910 and is surmounted by the family's avian emblem in the form of an ostrich-shaped weather vane.

Pageant Gardens were presented to the town on 5 September 1906 in memory of John Kenelm Digby

*Fincken's corn and seed merchants, on the east side of Cheap Street, in 1900.*

Wingfield-Digby, MP, who represented North Dorset from 1892 until his death on Christmas Day in 1904. A keen rider, he had bred most of his own hunters and carriage horses in the stables at Sherborne Castle. Pageant Gardens, with a mixture of lawns and trees including a 50-foot swamp cypress, are laid out around a bandstand in the curve of Digby Road between the former Digby Hotel and Sherborne Station. Until the First World War, Sherborne Town Band played in their Edwardian bandstand, in their fine braided uniform. It was a regular gathering throughout the summer on Wednesday evenings. As well as the military music there were visiting concert parties and a mixture of local amateur talent. These entertainers included the Lowman Brothers, Henry Durrant, Billy Brown and George Spiller.

The town's industrial name of the past two centuries bowed out in 1907 with Westbury Silk Mill, operated by generations of the Willmott family, being sold to woollen manufacturer A.R. Wright and his son, Arnold Wright, from Bingley.

Mary, Princess of Wales, the future Queen Mary, visited Sherborne School on 15 October 1908 and was given a military guard of honour.

Frederick Brooke Westcott, the headmaster of Sherborne School since 1892, retired in the spring of 1909 and was due to be replaced by Revd Charles Henry Thursfield Wood. Shortly after arriving Wood became seriously ill and died in May 1909. Studies might have been interrupted but games continued as before. 'Hacking in the grovel,' in Harry Hammond House's time at Sherborne, at the turn of the century, was the expression for 'booting-up the scrum' in a game of rugby.

The first telegraphic message to be wired from Longburton to Sherborne, in 1909, showed that at their inception, modern methods of communication were firmly in the control of persons of education: '*Nuntius aligeris hodie fulgoribus actus/Incipit hinc nostrum transvolitare polum.*' Which, for the enlightenment of the rest of us, translates thus: 'A message hence, by winged lightnings driven,/Today begins to fly across our heaven.'

Mary Ann Bull was the gypsy reddle woman of North Dorset in the early-twentieth century. She travelled, along with her wares and worldly goods, in a two-wheeled cart that was drawn by a small cream pony. A collie dog was chained to the axle. They slept rough beside the road.

Her round included most of the farms in the Sherborne, Shaftesbury and Sturminster Newton districts. There she sold reddle, the red dye for sheep marking and general coloration to make them more attractive at agricultural shows, and silver-sand which was an abrasive cleaner used to burnish steel mouth-tackle and stirrup irons.

In return she soaked up hospitality, particularly the rough cider that was made at just about every farm, and was frequently found sleeping it off underneath her cart. Once, however, the Oborne beat policeman found her drunk in charge and weaving about the highway. He tethered pony and collie and requisitioned a wheelbarrow for the conveyance of Miss Bull, whom he then pushed into Sherborne. The following day she was before the bench and fined, shouting back to the presiding magistrate: 'I suppose this is ten shillings for that bloody wheelbarrow man!' Mary Ann Bull died a few years later, in the manner in which she would have wished, beneath her cart at the roadside.

*Conduit* **(left)** *and cart with a policeman on the opposite pavement* **(below right-hand blind)** *in a view northwards up Cheap Street in 1904.*

# Cheap Street

*Typical high-street names, including Woolworths (left), Boots (centre) and Bollom (right), in a view southwards down Cheap Street from the junction with Abbey Road (bottom right).*

**Above:** *Roof-scape of the entire length of Cheap Street, northwards from the Long Street junction (bottom) to the buildings beside the Green (top), in a view from the Terrace.*

**Background:** *Looking down on South Street (foreground) and Cheap Street (centre) in a view of Sherborne and its setting northwards from the Terrace to pine woods on Ambrose Hill.*

**Above:** *The fifteenth-century Hospice of St Julian, known as the Julian on the Green (centre), facing the junction of Cheap Street and the Green with sixteenth-century buildings adjoining (right).*

**Right:** *The top end of Cheap Street, seen from Georgian bow-windows beside the Newland junction (left), south-westwards to the Greyhound Hotel and a fish-and-chip shop (centre).*

Left: *Shoemaker's House, from the south-east in 1995, with Oxford's bakery next door* (right).

Below left: *Shoemaker's House, on the west side of the street, after removal of its nine-teenth-century façade in 1994 to reveal its fifteenth-century timbers.*

Below: *Southwards down the west side of Cheap Street from Oxford's bakery* (right) *to half-timbered Shoemaker's House, New Look and Hardy's, in 1995.*

Below: *Looking down on the town from the Terrace, to Cheap Street* (right) *and the Methodist Church* (centre), *with Abbey House behind* (centre left) *and the Yeatman Hospital beyond* (top left).

Above: *The full fifteenth-century frontage of Shoemaker's House with the antique silver of trader Henry Willis in the left-hand window.*

Above: *Down the west side of Cheap Street in 1995 from the fishmonger (right) and Balfour News (centre) to the Little Art Shoppe, Blackmore Vale Travel and Humberts (left).*

Above: *Southwards down Cheap Street, from between Glovers of Sherborne (left) and the Little Art Shop (right) to a banner (centre) advertising the Christmas pantomime in 1984.*

Left: *The centre of Cheap Street, looking southwards to the tree-covered slopes, beyond the banner for Aladdin at the Digby Hall in December 1984.*

*Eighteenth-century frontage of the former Swan Hotel (centre left), facing sixteenth-century moulded braces over the entrance to Marney's (right) in a view south down central Cheap Street in 1984.*

Left: *The east side of central Cheap Street is dominated by the Ham stone façade of the Post Office, built c.1850, seen from the south-west in 2000 with pedestrians reclaiming the highway.*

Far left: *The west side of Cheap Street from watchmakers S.J. Grange Ltd, the shop front hiding a much older building, northwards in 1984.*

Below: *Puddles in Swan Yard, looking eastwards from Cheap Street on Christmas Day in 1984, to the Swan Steak Bar (centre).*

Below: *Half-timbered Abbeylands (left) and the west side of Cheap Street, looking north-westwards, on Christmas Day in 1984.*

Left: *Tudor-built Abbeylands which was sold to Sherborne School by John Cutler, the grandson of a former headmaster, in 1919.*

Below: *Pastiche version of a sixteenth-century house, rebuilt in the 1960s for what is now the National Westminster Bank, on the south side of the junction of Abbey Road (right) and Cheap Street (left).*

Bottom: *The Swan (left) and Dewhurst butchers, southwards down Cheap Street in 1984, from beside the overhanging half-timbered first floor of Abbeylands (right).*

Above: *Pavement view outside Woolworths (left), southwards down the west side of Cheap Street from Bollom (right) and the Pipe Shop (centre) to the wine merchants and Melson Wingate opticians.*

Top right: *Barclays Bank, on the corner of Cheap Street (left) and Hound Street (right), from the south in 1984.*

Above: *The path into the 1841-built Methodist Church on the west side of Cheap Street between the 1851-built shop fronts of T.E. Gillard, tobacconist, and W.H.R. Newcombe, clockmaker, seen from the east in 1984.*

Left: *Cheap Street, southwards and downwards, from the Swan Steak Bar (left) to South Street (centre right).*

Right: *The Pipe Shop of tobacconist T.E. Gillard and the religious notice-board (left), both of which survived a Luftwaffe bomb that dropped in the middle of Cheap Street, seen from the north-east in 1984.*

Left: *Methodist graveyard and buildings to the north in Abbey Road.*

Below: *Lamp-lit gates to the Methodist Church, now shared with the United Reform Church, open for worship on Christmas Day in 1984.*

Below left: *The view from the Methodist Church steps, westwards to Cheap Street in 1984.*

*East side of central Cheap Street, southwards from the junction with Hound Street (left), down to South Street in 1984.*

  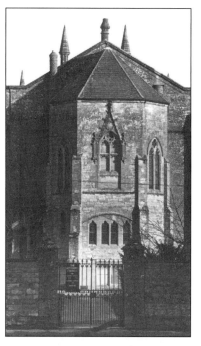

*Sequence of shop fronts, including Boots (left), Palmer Snell, Constance Wood, Hilton's, Lloyd's Bank, Bristol and West and Johnsons of Sherborne, as the east side of Cheap Street descends into South Street in 1984.*

*Ionic columns, Venetian window and railed balcony in the 1818-built bowed frontage of Sherborne's most elegant shop, at the north end of the Parade, which used to house the Sherborne Bank for Saving.*

*Rear view of the Methodist Church, looking east, towards its chimney, air-vent and pinnacles.*

Below: *The Abbey Bookshop, with a printing works above in an 1842-built three-storey house in the Parade, and the bowed frontage of the Southern Electricity showroom seen again from the east in 1984.*

*The Market Place and the Parade, looking north-westwards on Boxing Day in 1984.*

Above: *West side of central Cheap Street, southwards from the junction with Hound Street (left), to the Conduit in 1984.*

Above right: *Shops at the south end of the Parade on the west side of Cheap Street, 1984.*

Right: *Market Place, Conduit and SS Johns' Building (centre, built by the Almshouse Trust in 1894), and the Parade.*

Above: *An eighteenth-century house opposite the Parade, incorporating Victoria Wine (left) and Carter's Chemist (centre, est. 1790), with early-Victorian windows looking eastwards, 1984.*

Left: *Victoria Wine and Sherborne Pharmacy on the east side of Cheap Street in a view south-eastwards to the junction with Long Street (centre) and the Market Place (right).*

*Shops along the lower east side of Cheap Street (left), southwards to the Long Street junction and South Street, from Country Casuals (left) to Johnson's of Sherborne (centre).*

Above: *The Parade, 1999, from the Three Wishes (left) and Abbey Bookshop (centre) to Pavilion (right) in the former Southern Electricity showroom.*

Above right: *The Conduit from the Parade, looking south-eastwards to a backdrop of the newly-built Midland Bank on the corner with South Street and Long Street, with two members of the Ricketts family in the foreground in 1930.*

Right: *The Four Seasons in Georgian plaster, moulded for the dining-room of Sherborne Pharmacy.*

Below: *The east side of Cheap Street from Lloyd's Bank (left), southwards to Sherborne Pharmacy (centre) and South Street, with the Conduit (centre right) and Market Place on the other side of the road.*

*Conduit view, westwards into Church Lane, across a Market Place living up to its name in 1972.*

*The Conduit and 1894-built SS Johns' Building by lamp-light, southwards from Cheap Street.*

*Conservative Club (left), dated 1658, and Bow House (right) which was the Sun Inn until it was bought by Sherborne School for its Senior Common Room in 1916, looking westwards from Market Place into Church Lane (centre).*

## Seventeen

# 1910–1919

A seminal work, prophetic given its timing, was the treatise on *Machine-Gun Tactics* which appeared in 1910. Its author, Major Reginald Vincent Kempenfeldt Applin (1869–1957), was at Sherborne School from 1883 to 1886. He had joined the British North Borneo Service as a cadet in 1889 and saw action in the Syed and Mat Salleh rebellions from 1895 to 1897. He won the Distinguished Service Order as District Commissioner of Bloemfontein in the South African War. Applin took his own handbook into the field at Messines and Passchendaele in the great conflict to come, survived to leave the forces as Lieutenant-Colonel, and was the Conservative Member for Enfield, in Parliament, from 1924 to 1935. He retired to Natal.

Rawson Hall, named for its benefactor from Brecon House in Long Street, was the base for the Church Lads Brigade but in 1911 it was taken over on Saturdays for the first regular cinematograph shows in Sherborne. Mrs Hamblin played the piano continuously throughout the silent movie films as George Coombs worked the hand-turned projector. It was immediately popular and performances ran from two o'clock in the afternoon through to eleven o'clock at night. Prices were 6d. or 9d. for adults and 3d. for children. Later, Percy Coker opened Sherborne's first purpose-built cinema in Cheap Street, next to McGann's stationers, and in the 1930s a larger picture house was built in Newland.

Eldest son of the gardener at Sherborne Castle, an old boy of Foster's School, Sir George Pragnall (1863–1912) was knighted in King George V's birthday honours of 1912. As chairman of the National Patriotic Association and the Employers' Territorial Association he devised a way of preparing working men for war. In all 2,000 firms adopted the scheme in which, in return for three weeks' paid holiday, employees agreed to attend Territorial Army Camps for 14 days.

The first recorded flights of an aeroplane over Sherborne were by Herbert Spencer, the winner of aviation competitions at Brooklands, who arrived at the Conservative Fête in Sherborne Park on 5 August 1912. A huge crowd gathered around his biplane and turned into an orderly queue – largely left on the ground – as he took up a few brave and lucky passengers. They were carried one at a time on short circuits as far as the Abbey and the Old Castle.

In August 1914, at the declaration of war, B-Squadron of the Queen's Own Dorset Yeomanry mustered in Long Street. For many it would be their first experience not only of warfare but of exotic lands. They were destined for the Kasen-il Barracks on the Nile, at Cairo, and would later be attached to the British Expeditionary Force for the ill-fated Gallipoli landings, intended to oust the Turks from the Dardanelles. From there, re-formed with more recruits from home, the Dorset Yeomanry made a famous cavalry charge against Senussi warriors of the Moslem sect from the Sahara Desert. As I write, acting as my stage-prop for the day, I have a medieval-looking Senussi sword that was brought home to Sherborne, having been captured in that action on 26 November 1916. It is a souvenir from one of the last major engagements of its kind. The Dorset Yeomanry went on to join the Palestine offensive under General Sir Edmund Allenby. A chunky relic from that campaign, a Turkish field gun, stands outside the stables at Sherborne Castle.

Nowell Charles Smith (1871–1961), a housemaster from Winchester College, had been appointed headmaster of Sherborne School in 1909. A poetical biographer, on William Wordsworth and Sir Philip Sidney, he turned his attention to sermons on 'the riddles of the universe which have haunted man from the beginning.' His ambition for Sherborne was to 'put back the clock by turning an indifferent boarding establishment into a nation in miniature that is worthy of its origins as one of the first English public schools.' In setting about restoring the reputation of Sherborne School he was rewarded by the doubling of its roll – from 200 to 400 – by the time he left in 1927. One of those boys, however, turned into the bane of his life.

For many years after 1917 there was an old-boy's book that never appeared on the library shelves of Sherborne School. This appeared as Fernhurst in *The Loom of Youth* by Alec Waugh (1898–1981) which was written in seven and a half weeks, during the First World War, when he was a 17-year-old pupil. Alec, the elder brother of Evelyn Waugh, saw it as a 'love letter to Sherborne' and sought to break that great taboo – 'the conspiracy of silence' – surrounding schoolboy relationships.

The book had to be completed in haste in December 1915 as Alec Waugh was due to sail to Flanders to fight in the trenches. 'Surely you will fight for King and Country,' was the last poster he saw in the London Underground, urging 'Come along, Boys, before it is too late.' Alec posted the manuscript to his father, the Shirburnian author, critic and editor Arthur Waugh, at Underhill, North

End Road, Hampstead. He was the managing director of Chapman and Hall and had just published *Reticence in Literature*. Arthur saw Alec's novel into print in 1917:

*Just after Christmas in 1915 he began* The Loom of Youth, *writing it on any odd sheets of paper which he could collect in the hut of the YMCA at Berkhamsted, and sending me the pages to read, morning after morning, between breakfast time and the next parade. He wrote the book with the conviction of a man who had a task set before him, and he carried the task through within a period of six weeks. It was a genuine tour de force, done against time.*

Textual inconsistencies, such as having the trains for Derbyshire pulling out of Waterloo, resulted from the publisher making last-minute changes to the 300 pages of proofs to lessen the chances of a libel action. The headmaster of Fernhurst is Talbot Baines Reed and the school is said to need just two reforms – dismissal of all the masters and expulsion of all the boys. Alec by now was serving with the Dorsetshire Regiment on the Western Front and was taken prisoner of war in 1918. Those who risked life and limb to contend with daily hazards such as a runaway cart in Cheap Street borrowed the language of war to denounce him as 'a traitor to School and Country, despicably unpatriotic'.

Despite the rhetoric, the novel contains no explicit sexual references, and by the standards of the end of the century seemed quite restrained. It would have been more accurate to have described it as subversive. To the uninitiated, or those from a non-public-school background, it was regarded as a celebration of cricket. Alec Waugh's boyfriend was named Arthur. Both were caught and Alec was expelled. Their book was banned in Sherborne and boys were promised an immediate beating if they were caught in possession of a copy. As a result, driven underground, it became required reading. 'Put house and school above your personal desires,' Nowell Smith urged, as he issued an edict forbidding associations between boys of different houses, or with those of a different age.

Parkstone youngster David John Moore Cornwell (born 1931), from the next generation of Shirburnians, put Carne School into his thriller *A Murder of Quality* in 1962. Whether it is an allusion to 'Cerne' or 'carnal' is for spy-master George Smiley to determine. The school's Digby accommodation, in the former Digby Hotel, features as the Sawley Arms. Writing as John le Carre, he describes the school as seething in class corruption and as 'a sanatorium of dying souls'. Despite those reservations, it proves an excellent start in life for several of his characters. He returns to school in *A Perfect Spy*. John Cowper Powys also made use of the Digby Hotel, as the Lovelace Hotel, in *Wolf Solent*.

Building work at Sherborne School to designs by Sir Reginald Blomfield included the Carrington Buildings of 1910 and classrooms in 1913. The decade saw many additions including Lyon House in 1911 and Far Field in 1913. As the world went to war, on 4 August 1914, former members of Sherborne School Cadet Force and others who trained in the Volunteers' Drill Hall in Acreman Street enlisted in their hundreds. What awaited them, in terms of duration and the advent of aerial and chemical warfare, was unlike any other conflict in history. Even the traditional sort of operation kept going fearfully wrong. Lieutenant-Colonel A. Kearsey of the 5th Battalion of the Dorsetshire Regiment sent home an upbeat assessment of landings in the Mediterranean which the First Lord of the Admiralty, Winston Churchill, had conceived as 'a bayonet into the soft under-belly of the Turk': 'Rested, recuperated, and reinforced, the men are now fit and strong, and full of work and hope.'

Reality was very different. Their secret evacuation from the Gallipoli misadventure in the Dardanelles was masterminded by Old Shirburnian General Sir Charles Munro. He arrived in Sherborne as an 11-year-old, from Australia, in 1871. In the First World War he commanded the 2nd Division in 1914 and the 3rd Army in 1915 before 'being handed the poisoned chalice of Commander-in-Chief Eastern Mediterranean.'

His despatch to London sealed the death-knell to Winston Churchill's bold initiative. Even if the forces pinned down in the Dardanelles could secure their positions there was no possibility of an advance on Constantinople. Therefore, as no purpose was served by remaining, it was sensible to leave. The solution he devised for extricating the Allies from landing beaches under the enemy guns was to continue the appearance of normal working for as long as possible, whilst at the same time withdrawing all reserve forces and materials, and then to pull out 'remaining units as speedily as possible'. Having accustomed the Turks to long periods of inaction, during which 23,000 British and 4,000 French troops were withdrawn, the grand plan left 17,000 men to be evacuated on the final night.

They were defended by only one British 6-inch gun and six French heavy guns after leaving their trenches at 23.45 hours. Bad weather threatened to delay embarkation, but also covered what was happening, until 03.30 hours on 8 January 1916 as the last 160 men left West Beach at Helles and 'timed fuses set to stores and ammunition began to operate.' The lack of Turkish aerial observation helped to extricate the men without harassment from a campaign costly in British lives and prestige. Sir Charles Munro could hardly be given battle honours but he had saved thousands of brave men 'to live and fight another day'.

Sherborne teacher Gwyon Lloyd – 'a kind, simple-minded giant' – had been killed there by a Turkish bullet as he stepped ashore at Suvla Bay. Another teacher, international hockey player J.Y. Robinson, was shot through the spine and lay paralysed for six months before he died. And 19-year-old Second-Lieutenant E.G. Templeman Kitson from Beaminster, a member of Sherborne School's shooting VIII who had represented them at Bisley in 1913 and 1914, died from his wounds on 3 September 1916.

The equivalent of the whole school roll of that time were wiped out in the First World War – 221 old Shirburnians fell during the conflict – which was an attrition rate of nearly 20 per cent. A total of 1,157 ex-pupils of Sherborne School had served in the Armed Forces. Their honours included two Victoria Crosses, 58 Distinguished Service Orders, 76 Military Crosses, 101 other decorations and 137 mentions in despatches. Both Shirburnian VCs returned to tell their tales.

Major Edward Bamford VC, DSO (1887–1928), of the Royal Marines saw action in the Battle of Jutland on HMS *Royal Sovereign* and won his awards in the audacious attack with explosives-loaded ships that blockaded the port of Zeebrugge on 23 April 1918. His recreations were golf, hockey, tennis, sailing and fishing. Having survived the war, and being unmarried, he stayed in the Marines and went to Hong Kong as an instructor of small arms in 1926. He died there on 29 September 1928.

Brigadier Charles Edward Hudson, VC (1892–1959), also held the DSO and bar, MC, Croix de Guerre and the Italian silver medal for valour. His notable achievement with Sherborne School Cadet Corps was to win a house drill competition by duly responding to 'Fix bayonets' without having a bayonet in its sheath. Hudson was so adept at going through the motions that the adjudicator failed to notice its absence.

His Victoria Cross, from 1918, resulted from the same determination to turn a catastrophe into an achievement. Having been wrong-footed by a bomb, which left him limping, he recovered his composure and led a scratch detachment of 'cooks, orderlies and runners' in what should have been a suicidal counter-attack against advancing Germans. Lieutenant-Colonel Hudson commanded the Sherwood Foresters whose war became the extended version, continuing eastwards after the Armistice in 1918, with the following year spent supporting White Russian resistance against the Bolsheviks. Between the wars Hudson was chief instructor at the Royal Military College, Sandhurst, and in the next conflict he commanded the 2nd Infantry Brigade. He retired to Denbury Manor, Newton Abbot, Devon, where he was county commissioner of the St John Ambulance Brigade.

Brigadier Euston Edward Francis Baker DSO, MC and bar (1895–1981), joined the Middlesex Regiment on 15 August 1914 and served in France until 1919. His achievement, as Colonel of his regiment, was to lead its 2nd Battalion in the capture of Douai during the final British advance of October 1918. Captain of football and the School Eight, at Sherborne, it was always his ambition to join the Army. He had been rejected, however, on grounds of poor eyesight but fought back in the shooting championships at Bisley. When he won the Spencer Cup, in 1914, recruitment officers were forced to change their minds. He was ADC to King George VI from 1941.

Colonel Geoffrey Nowell Salmon (1871–1954) of the Rifle Brigade – as Private Salmon from Lyon House – was the bugler of the newly formed Sherborne School Cadet Force in 1888. He entered the Army in 1894 and served in the Boer War and the First World War. In the latter he was awarded the DSO, CMG and the American Distinguished Service Medal. He was the son of Admiral of the Fleet, Sir Nowell Salmon, VC (1835–1912), who won his Victoria Cross at the siege of Lucknow during the Indian Mutiny, in 1858.

Lieutenant-Colonel Roger Alvin Poore (1870–1917), remembered in Sherborne as a boxer, joined the Royal Wiltshire Yeomanry and won the Queen's Medal with seven clasps, in the Boer War, between 1899 and 1902. He stayed in South Africa, as resident magistrate in Transvaal and then Deputy Commissioner of the Police in Pretoria. He returned to Europe for the First World War, acting as second in command of the 2nd Royal Welch Fusiliers, and was awarded the Distinguished Service Order before being killed in France on 26 September 1917.

Captain Robert Kestell-Cornish joined the Dorsetshire Regiment. He was with a contingent from Sherborne that was inspected by Lord Kitchener, at an Officer Training Camp at Farnborough, in 1910. Having been gassed on Hill 60 on the Front Line on the night of 1 May 1915, he won the Military Cross for rallying the men who remained after their comrades had been asphyxiated. They managed to hold the summit until reinforcements arrived. He then won a bar to the MC for commanding a working party under heavy fire. The shells caught up with him in Houlthulst Forest in March 1918 and he died from his wounds in June that year. In the words of his headmaster:

*Many here will understand why at this moment the picture which fills my eye is that of Robert Kestell-Cornish, who died of his wounds only last Monday after a struggle of many weeks – our first winner or at any rate one of our first two winners of the Military Cross. As a boy here he was the very image of light hearted boyishness, and boyish at heart to the end, yet, within a few months of leaving school, playing the part of a man, a leader of men, a hero, in the very first onset and bewilderment of the newly invented devilry of a gas attack; and thereafter undertaking duties of leadership, decisions on which hung the issues of life and death for many others; and all at an age when in other times no more would have been expected of him than an intelligent pursuit of his studies, together with the innocent but irresponsible gaiety of an undergraduate.*

That story of an almost iconic casualty was matched by the survival of another remarkable boy. Captain Max Westlake (1895–1987) of the Royal Northumberland Fusiliers, came to Sherborne in 1910, excelled in boxing, and captained the first XI and also played for the first XV from 1912 to 1914. On returning to England from the Labour Corps in France he returned to Sherborne School and was a master, organising physical training, from 1923 until retirement in 1962. He became housemaster of Elmdene and then Abbey House – his own old house – for a total of 24 years. Old Shirburnian Michael McCrum, who became headmaster of Eton in 1970, recalled that Westlake survived long enough to search out showings across three counties of his favourite film – *The Sound of Music*. Fellow teacher Bob Powell gave an example of how with increasing maturity the stern regime he had maintained from before the First World War could occasionally be challenged at the edges: 'Do you mind, Chief, if we stop cold baths because the weather is so chilly?'

After he retired, Max Westlake put his energies and an old dark-brown Renault at the disposal of the Yeatman Hospital and its car service for patients.

Sherborne School, during the First World War, had 320 boys. The Digby Endowed School for Girls, dating from 1743, had 100 scholars of whom 14 were boarders. Foster's Endowed Grammar School in Hound Street, built in 1874, was operating as a secondary school under the Board of Education. Its distinguished old boy of the First World War was Lieutenant-Colonel Sir Arthur Adams (1861–1937), the son of a Sherborne jeweller, who sailed to Malaya and became Solicitor-General of Penang. As 'the white Rajah of the colony' he mobilised and commanded the Penang Volunteers for the duration of the colony.

Sherborne School for Girls, in Bradford Road, had a new extension which was opened by the Countess of Ilchester in July 1910. The Catholic school was St Anthony's Convent in Westbury.

Chairman of Sherborne Urban District Council, which had its offices in South Street, was Henry James Seager of the Newland glove-making family. Alexander Tutt was the Town Crier. Colonel John Robert Phelips Goodden of Compton House, Over Compton, chaired Sherborne Rural District Council.

The cottage opposite the Almshouse, at the junction of Westbury and Trendle Street, was George Hodges' Livery Stables. Six to eight ponies were stabled there at the end of a double passage. Until the 1920s they were on contract hire to the Post Office and hauled red two-wheeled Royal Mail traps between Sherborne Station and the Post Office.

Early-morning sorting of incoming mail completed, they headed out of town shortly after six o'clock, on deliveries. Part of the postman's job was to rest and feed his pony – as well as himself – for three hours at around midday. He then made the afternoon collections on his way back into Sherborne.

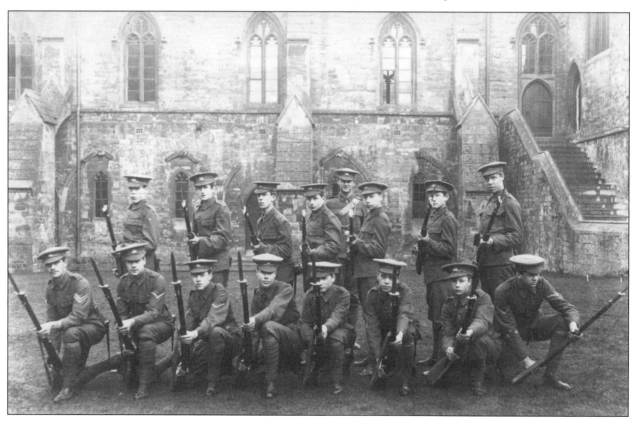

*Officer cadets at Sherborne School defending the Chapel steps before departing for the First World War.*

# The Green & Greenhill

*Greenhill (top left) and the Green, looking northwards from the top of Cheap Street into Higher Cheap Street (right), to the George Hotel and the Julian on the Green (far right).*

*Left: Georgian brick of c.1790, on the south side of the Green, given a restrained and traditional shop front when David Webb converted it into the Music House in 1970.*

Right: *Greenhill House on the south-west side of the Green, built in 1607 and regarded as the best seventeenth-century house in the town, was acquired for Sherborne School in 1960.*

*The sign of the White Hart (left) and the north-east side of the Green (centre) towards Higher Cheap Street (right).*

Above: *No. 3 The Green* (left) *eastwards to the George Yard* (centre) *and Julian on the Green* (right) *in 1997.*

Above: *The Green, with a nineteenth-century house fronted with ashlar* (centre) *but rubble-built at the side, looking northwards up Higher Cheap Street* (right).

Below: *North-eastwards from the Green to the George Inn and arched George Yard* (centre) *beside the projecting Ham stone walls of the medieval hospice named for St Julian of Norwich* (centre right).

Below: *The flag of England and Saint George, beside the sign of the George Hotel, in a view down Higher Cheap Street to the Julian* (centre) *in 1997.*

Left: *Thatched St Michael's* (left), *followed by the assertive Georgian bow-windows and finials of Alpine, thatched No. 3* (centre) *and the shop front of Country Pine and Antiques* (right) *in 1984.*

*Above left: The top of Greenhill in 1984 with the Antelope Hotel (left) and Seymour's wine-merchants (centre) with the latter perpetuating use of these buildings for licensed premises, including the King's Arms which was* previously known as the Globe Inn.

*Above right: South-facing frontage of the Antelope Hotel, a coaching inn replacing the Horseshoe hostelry, which opened on 11 April 1748 and hosted journal-writer Parson James Woodforde and friends for dinner on 4 August 1789.*

Above: *Ham stone of the Julian (left), sixteenth-century half-timbering of the building facing down Cheap Street (centre), and eighteenth-century brick at Country Chattels (right).*

Below: *Junction view, streaked by the lines of passing traffic on a timed-exposure, from the south end of Bristol Road to George Street (left), Greenhill Motor House and Higher Cheap Street beside it (right), 1984.*

**Ionic columns, fronting the eighteenth-century Antelope Hotel, south-westwards to the top of Greenhill.**

Left: *Mixed early-nineteenth-century roof styles of thatch, tile and slate along the central north-eastern side of the Green.*

Below: *The Green, acquired for Sherborne School by Lord Iliffe in 1929, which as the Angel Inn from 1750 carried the name of 'C. Johnson, Licensed to Let Post Horses'.*

Left: *Back Lane* (left), *fair-day stall facing the Green and the tree overhanging the bus shelter, looking north-westwards to Greenhill.*

Below: *The north side of Greenhill down from Cobblers* (right) *to Cumberland House, Downside, Old Forge Cottage, Quadring, Crofters, Helvetia, the Matchbox and Pendennis.*

Left: *Raised pavement and old cottages on the south side of Greenhill, the earliest with a 1664 date stone, looking south-west towards the headlight of an approaching motorcyclist (bottom right).*

Below: *Early-Victorian terraced houses on the north side of Greenhill facing the bus shelter and the roundabout.*

Left: *The Green building (left), formerly the Angel Inn, north-eastwards from the former Green open space (tarmac foreground) in 1984.*

Right: *By 1998 the Green building (right) was smothered in Virginia creeper – brought to England by Raleigh's traders – and is seen from a floral roundabout in a view north-east to the Antelope Hotel (left).*

Below: *Seventeenth-century stone mullioned windows of Priory House (left), the home of prolific author Horace Annesley Vachell, and the eighteenth-century brick of Camelot (right).*

Above right: *Priory House, on the northern side of Greenhill, dates back to the seventeenth century but its nineteenth-century doorway is dominated by a single immense Ham stone lintel (centre) incised with lines to make it look as if this single stone comprised separate blocks.*

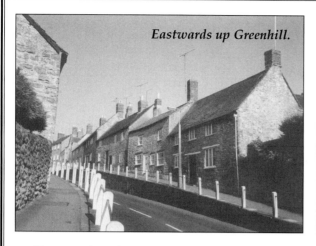

*Eastwards up Greenhill.*

**Above right:** *The south side of central Greenhill, in 1997, from Godden and Curtis* (left) *and the Pheasants Hotel, to eighteenth-century Pinehurst* (centre) *and aptly-named Gable House* (right).

**Above:** *Victorian house and Edwardian kindergarten on the north side of Greenhill, south-west of the Antelope Hotel.*

**Above:** *Crown Cottage, on the south side of central Greenhill, where the raised pavement is at its highest.*

**This image:** *South-westwards from the roundabout beside the Green, down Greenhill, towards a saturated south-western sky on Boxing Day in 1984.*

## Eighteen

### ✣
# *1920–1929*

The eminent architect William Douglas Caroe (1857–1938), whose Dorset work included Colehill Parish Church and South Lytchett Manor, rebuilt Sherborne School. He was president of the Architectural Association in 1895. His work at Sherborne continued to designs by Sir Reginald Blomfield (1856–1942), including the War Memorial staircase of 1922, the imposing stone Tower and wooden Gymnasium of 1923, and a Music School in 1926. Other additions included Westcott House in 1920, Bow House and the Workshop in 1921, the Chapel memorial extension in 1922, and the Gateway in 1923.

That year the school cadet corps had to put up with being inspected 'by a mere colonel' but for the boys and town there was the excitement of a royal visit, by the 29-year-old Prince of Wales – the future King Edward VIII – on 19 July 1923. There was also another day to remember. G.M. Garrett, who was in School House from 1921 to 1926, recalled a cadet march past in which many of the boys 'took the Mickey' and held up their fingers to the Regimental Sergeant Major. Prefect T.L. Binney failed to identify all the culprits and decided to beat all the contingent from School House:

*Plinth of the newly erected War Memorial, in the former Abbey churchyard, smothered with wreaths on Armistice Day, 1922.*

*We did not believe we would be beaten but we certainly were. Each one received four full-blooded strokes – all 60 of us. He broke four canes, took most of the skin off the inside of his right hand, and acquired legendary status of the holder of a record never likely to be broken.*

Another record, off his own bat, was achieved by A.W. Carr – later to be captain of England's cricketers – when he scored over 300 runs in an innings against a Dorset amateur side. The setting was King's School playing-fields, at Horsecastles, to a backdrop of the splendid Victorian pavilion with its lofty clock tower.

Shirburnian athlete, Hyla Bristow Stallard (1901–73), from Lyon House, ran the mile for Great Britain in the Olympic Games of 1924 which were held in London. He went on to become one of the distinguished eye surgeons of his time. The author of *Eye Surgery*, he became president of the Opthalmalogical Society of the United Kingdom.

Prolific (which is something of an understatement) Horace Annesley Vachell (1861–1955) of the Priory House at Sherborne spent all of his long adult life writing, from the *Romance of Judge Ketchum* (1894) to *Quests* 60 years later. By then he had just about reached his ambition of 100 titles and came reasonably close to celebrating his own centenary. Many of the works are plays. *Her Son* was also turned into a novel. The story *Quinney's*, on the other hand, was dramatised in 1915. Other plays included *Count X* (1921) and *Plus Fours* (1923). Vachell was also an essayist, with *My Vagabondage* (1936), *Little Tyrannies* (1940) and *A Writer's Autobiography*. The best known of his novels are *Whitewash* (1920), *Quinney's Adventures* (1924), *Vicar's Walk* (1933) and *Quinneys for Quality* (1938). There are many allusions to Sherborne in his work and the spiritualist story *The Other Side* (1910) is set in the town.

Traditionally, at midnight on the eve of Pack Monday Fair (which is held on 10 October if it falls on a Monday or the first Monday thereafter) the people of Sherborne take to the streets in a noisy procession called Teddy Roe's Band. It gathers at Greenhill, at the top end of Cheap Street, and then winds around town – or did so until it was restrained by the police. Its origins lay, it was claimed, in a celebration of the Abbey craftsmen in the Middle Ages. They beat their tools against buckets to maximise the noise. Attempts were made in the late-twentieth century to keep the custom going in a socially acceptable form but Victor Swatridge, a Sherborne policeman of the 1920s, remembered the event being used as an excuse for primitive tribalism:

*The inhabitants of Sherborne relentlessly followed this custom and the noise emitted in the still dark hours of the early morning was hideous and frightening. It eventually developed into rather riotous behaviour and a kind of feud existed, sections of the crowd would break up and go in various directions, vengeance was wrought on people who were borne a grudge against, resulting in windows of shops and houses being smashed and gardens trampled over and virtually ruined.*

# Long Street

West along Long Street to its junction with Cheap Street at the centre of the town with the Conduit, Market Place and Sherborne Abbey (straight ahead) in 1965.

Junction view, from Cheap Street eastwards, showing the northern side of Long Street (left) to the junction with St Swithin's Road.

Left: Long Street and the Cheap Street junction in a study of roofs and pinnacles on Boxing Day in 1984.

Background: Eastwards along Long Street, from Sherborne Abbey, to the former Sherborne Brewery (top corner) and the Old Castle (beyond).

Right: Tudor timbers, part of a frontage dating from 1500, preserved at the west end of Long Street beside the South Street junction, when the remainder of the building was demolished in 1926.

Church House

School

Below: *The eighteenth-century Abbot's Litten* (left) *and sixteenth-century Pretor's Office* (centre) *and Bank House* (right), *from the north-east in 1984.*

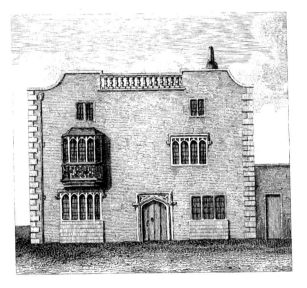

**Eastwards along the south side of Long Street from Castle House (centre) to the former Sherborne Brewery (left).**

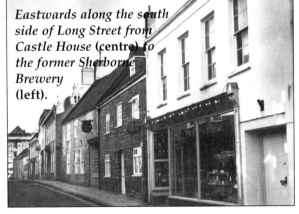

Left: *The north side of Long Street from Hunt's Cycle Works* (left) *and medieval Tudor Rose with the early-nineteenth-century shop window* (centre) *eastwards to the China Gallery and Edwin Childs and Son's garage* (right) *in 1984.*

Right: *House on the north side of Long Street, between Childs' Garage* (left) *and railings of the Congregational Church* (right), *1984.*

Above: *Westwards along the south side of Long Street from the ashlar-faced Abbot's Litten (left) and Pretor's Office of the Sherborne and Dorsetshire Bank (centre) to Sherborne Abbey (right of centre).*

Above right: *Sherborne Brewery (left), seen after conversion into flats with Langside, Tintern and Rosedale to the west, from the steps into the 1852-built Congregational schoolroom.*

Right: *Early-nineteenth-century Cromwell House (left), Belmont and Wisteria House, northwards from the entrance to Culverhayes car park.*

Left: *Eighteenth-century stone mullions and drip stones on the north side of the west end of Long Street, beside the Ramsbury Building Society, in 1984.*

Above: *The fortress-like Sherborne Brewery (bottom right), operated by the Dorsetshire Brewery Co. (Sherborne) Ltd from 1796, is second only to Sherborne Abbey in terms of size. Also known as Baxter's Brewery, Sherborne Brewery was renamed the Maltings on being converted into luxury flats in 1984.*

# Nineteen

# 1930-1939

The little brick kiosk on the north side of Half Moon Street, outside the Abbey, was Brett's Weighbridge. Corn merchant Cecil Benjamin Brett, who retired to Wilton in Newland, was succeeded on Abbey Corner in Digby Road by Gerald Cecil Brett. Until about 1930 the weighbridge was in regular use for the local grain crop as well as coal and coke which had been brought in by rail. The building has a remarkable Ham stone doorway with the jambs and lintel carved from a single block of stone. This has suffered weathering but there are still traces of the frieze of leaves that decorated the top. The metal bridge apparatus was removed when the road was widened in the 1950s.

The Carlton in Newland, managed by Edgar Billett, was Sherborne's first purpose-built 'Picture Palace' (tel. Sherborne 161). It played to packed houses as silent films gave way to 'the talkies'. There was even a local report on the newsreels. Sherborne was sometimes in the news, such as when PM Ramsay Macdonald dined at the Digby Hotel in 1932.

In 1933, having been owned by Sherborne School for several centuries, the Conduit in Cheap Street was handed over by its trustees to the town. It had been scheduled as an ancient monument, at the instigation of Dorset Field Club, in 1928.

Convicted arsenic murderer Charlotte Bryant (1903–36) was hanged on what would now be exposed and rejected as flawed evidence. The story came to national attention after her husband Frederick Bryant died on Sunday 22 December 1935 at Coombe Farm, Castleton, in the valley east of the B3148, Marston Magna road, a mile north of Sherborne (ST 621 184). Suspicions were aroused because he had suffered gastric pains since May that year.

Attention centred on his wife, whom he had met in her home town of Londonderry, where he was serving with the Dorsetshire Regiment during the Troubles and Partition, in 1922. Charlotte was not coping and on 31 December 1935 she was taken into care at the Public Assistance Institution in Sturminster Newton – now Stour View House (ST 787 148) – and on 10 February was placed in custody and charged with murder.

The trial of Charlotte Bryant was held at the Assize Court in Shire Hall, High West Street, Dorchester, in May 1936. Her closest friend from Sherborne, Lucy Ostler, said that she was called to the cottage in Coombe when Frederick was dying. She was asked to stay and fell asleep in a cot in the room: 'The next thing I heard was Charlotte asking her husband if he had it because I heard him vomiting afterwards.' Two days after his death, Charlotte pointed to a small green tin in a cupboard and said: 'I must get rid of that.' Lucy Ostler next saw it a couple of days later when she cleared the grate in the copper: 'I threw it on the rubbish tip in the garden.' There police found the remains of a tin which contained traces of rat poison. It had been bought from a Yeovil chemist. Dr Roche Lynch, an expert in toxicology who was lecturing at two London teaching hospitals, told the court:

*I submitted ashes taken from the gate behind the copper to technical analysis. I found they contained 149 parts to the million of arsenic. This is so abnormally large a proportion, it indicates something containing arsenic must have been burnt in that grate.*

Mrs Bryant denied the charge and her trial lasted four days. The jury returned in an hour with a verdict of 'guilty' and Mr Justice Mackinnon pronounced the death sentence. On appeal, evidence from Professor William A. Bone of Imperial College of Science and Technology was presented by the defence, showing that the arsenic content of house coal is never less than 140 parts per million and can exceed 1,000 parts. Lord Chief Justice Hewart rejected the new evidence and denounced forensic science:

*The court will not listen to the opinions of scientific gentlemen bringing their minds to bear on evidence which they have not heard. Moreover it is clear that there has been no mistake.*

Gordon Hewart, 1st Baron Hewart (1870–1943), 'a member of many Masonic lodges', was very much a political member of the judiciary. Having been Solicitor-General and then Attorney-General, he served as a Cabinet minister, and was one of the signatories of the Irish Peace Treaty in 1921. It may be relevant to note, in this context, that Charlotte was Derry-born. Concern was expressed in Parliament that a woman was about to hang on discredited technical evidence. It was pointed out that there had been no confession. Nor was there any compelling medical evidence. Witnesses had contributed nothing more than hearsay and suspicions. The Home Secretary, Sir John Simon, created 1st Viscount Simon (1873–1954) told MPs that the appeal judge assumed that Dr Lynch had made a mistake, but considered that the verdict had been sound. Therefore, he said, the sentence had to stand. Charlotte Bryant was duly hanged.

# Southern Town
## South Street

Above: *Northwards along South Street* (centre) *from the Slopes with a train passing through Sherborne on 15 December 1984.*

Above: *No. 21 South Street, down by the level-crossing, during renovation in 1997.*

Above: *South Street south-wards from the Conduit* (right) *and Market Place to the Midland Bank on the corner with Long Street* (left) *and Denner's* (centre) *in the former Phillips and Son's drapery store rebuilt after wartime bombing.*

Left: *South Street* (right), *photographed from the Terrace by Adam Gosney in about 1914, looking north-westwards over 1863-dated Sherborne Gas Works to Sherborne Station, Pageant Gardens* (centre) *and the Digby Hotel.*

## Ludbourne Road

Left: *The north-west corner of the supermarket complex, looking south from Ludbourne Road into South Street* (right).

Below: *J. Sainsbury's supermarket, seen in the evening sun in 1997, dominates Ludbourne Road.*

Above: *Sidewalk offer* (bottom left) *at the cathedral of commerce.*

Left: *Towering name – the highest of the supermarket logos.*

Below, left: *Sign of the former Fire Station in Ludbourne Road.*

Below: *Skateboarding street art on the door to the old Fire Station in 1997.*

119

## Church Close

*Southwards along Church Close, facing the former Abbey churchyard, from the Cottage (right) in 1984.*

## Church Lane

*Stepping out from the Abbey, eastwards into Church Lane (left), towards the Sue Ryder Shop which the generation at the time of writing remembers as Macnally's newsagents and our predecessors as Dick Tuffin's Tuck Shop.*

*Eastwards from Sherborne Museum (right) to fifteenth-century Bow Arch and the Market Place (centre) beyond the wall of the medieval Abbey precinct.*

*The western end of Church Lane, looking northwards into the passage between the Chapel of St Mary le Bow (left) and former Macnally's newsagents, seen as a Sue Ryder Shop in 2000.*

*Digby Road*

Above: *The 1884-built Digby Memorial* (centre foreground) *and Digby Road* (left) *in a view south-westwards to the former Digby Hotel* (towards top left) *and the skyline from the Terrace west to the 519-foot summit of Honeycombe Wood* (right of centre).

Left: *Pageant Gardens in 1997, looking south-westwards from Digby Road to a fine swamp cypress* (right) *and the bandstand* (left).

Right: *The Half Moon Field, here newly laid out as Pageant Gardens, having been given to the town by Major Frederick James Bosworth Wingfield Digby in memory of his father and named to commemorate the town's Edwardian Pageant which was held at the Old Castle.*

*Bandstand in Pageant Gardens, in a view northwards to Sherborne Abbey* (centre).

## Trendle Street

This image: *Trendle Street, eastwards from the junction with Acreman Street and Horsecastles (foreground), glimpsing Sherborne Abbey (left skyline) and the gable-end of the Almshouse (centre).*

Top right: *Resident steps out from the sunny side of Trendle Street, next door to Fishers (right).*

Right: *Quatrefoil panel, probably from the ruins of All Hallows Church, re-set in the wall of the seventeenth-century Corner House on the junction of Trendle Street and Acreman Street.*

## Westbury

Left: *Frontage of the Britannia Inn from the east.*

Below: *Westbury, and the inn, south-westwards.*

Centre bottom: *The Britannia Inn was formerly a school, as is recorded by the stone plaque above the door (right).*

Bottom left: *Britannia Inn entrance and inscription (top) for the school founded here by William, Lord Digby, in 1743.*

## Hound Street

Left: *Booklore* (centre) *from the east, in a view towards the Cheap Street junction, in 1984.*

Right: *West along Hound Street towards Cheap Street* (centre).

Below: *Eastwards along Hound Street with Booklore* (right) *advertising its Christmas catalogue in 1984.*

## Half Moon Street

Left: *Built in 1530 and now divided into shops, Church House (left) extends in long-house style along the north side of Half Moon Street, eastwards to South Street (right).*

Below: *Spring-time view of the west end of Church House, showing its south-facing frontage, housing the Aldous Collection in 1997.*

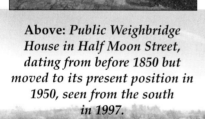

**Above:** *Public Weighbridge House in Half Moon Street, dating from before 1850 but moved to its present position in 1950, seen from the south in 1997.*

**Background:** *Half Moon Street (foreground) from the Abbey with the Plume of Feathers (bottom left) and pet and garden suppliers C.B. Brett and Son, followed by Digby Road junction and T.E. Vincent's Supply Stores (centre) which evolved from being the Victorian town's primary grocery shop into a Gateway supermarket.*

**Above left:** *The rear of the Half Moon Hotel, rebuilt in 1936, in Half Moon Street, is seen from the south.*

*Twenty*

✤

# *1940–1949*

One of the last great secrets of the Second World War centred on the work of a brilliantly talented old Shirburnian, mathematician Alan Turing (1912–54), who did more to save his country in the twentieth century than all the rest of his famous predecessors did in their generations. Unkempt and unconventional, Turing devised the world's first programmed digital computers, known as 'Turing Machines' (or 'Türing Machines' under the mistaken assumption that someone so devilishly clever had to be German). He created the 'Turing Bombe' to crack the cipher codes of the polyalphabetic enemy cryptographic enigma teleprinter-enciphering machines which scrambled German military radio communications into a form they wrongly assumed would remain unbreakable.

The work was carried out in the Government Code and Cipher School at Bletchley Park, Buckinghamshire, and itself became the 'Ultra Secret' of the war. The source of the Bletchley information, being the Germans themselves, had to be kept secret at all costs for the duration of the conflict. Cover stories disguised the source of the intelligence surfeit the military was enjoying and acting upon, to prevent the existence of the 'geese who laid the golden eggs and never cackled' – Churchill's phrase – from being known to either allies or enemies. The same obsessive secrecy prevailed into the Cold War and prevented public recognition of Turing's importance and role during his own lifetime.

Deciphering the Luftwaffe codes came first, for the benefit of Spitfire pilots like Shirburnian Squadron Leader Peter Devitt of 152 Squadron from RAF Warmwell, who took it personally that he was unable to stop his old school and town being devastated by bombs on 30 September 1940. Enigma decoding was as valuable as radar in thwarting the bombing campaign. In the Mediterranean theatre the Desert War turned as much on the cutting of Rommel's supply lines, by betraying the location and content of vital cargoes, as on the public victory at El Alamein.

The most difficult triumph for Turing's team of cryptanalysts was to break the new German naval codebook which was introduced on 1 February 1942. That came at a time when the Battle of the Atlantic might otherwise have been lost, because German U-boats were sinking ships faster than America could build them. Success at Bletchley saved the convoys and turned the northern ocean into a submarine graveyard. The quantity of the information was as great as its quality. Thousands of decrypts were produced at Bletchley each day.

Winston Churchill visited Bletchley and met Alan Turing. As a result, on 21 October 1941, Turing sent a list of demands in a personal memo to the Prime Minister who responded immediately and in full: 'Action this day. Make sure they have all they want on extreme priority and report to me that this has been done.'

Turing lacked in his personality all of the mathematical certainties with which he played in his mind. He was a homosexual contributor to his nation's fortunes who more than balanced out those Cambridge homosexuals who were betraying their country with conscienceless ease. Turing's private life could not be as tightly concealed as his official secrets. One of his happier moments was a return to Sherborne School, on 9 March 1953, which he described in a letter to his mother:

*Went down to Sherborne to lecture some boys on computers. Really quite a treat, in many ways. They were so luscious, and so well mannered, with a little dash of pertness, and Sherborne itself quite unspoilt.*

Alan Turing had been convicted in 1952 of gross indecency with another male. In 1953 he was implanted with oestrogen to render him impotent. On what his biographer, Andrew Hodges, describes as 'the coldest and wettest Whit Monday for fifty years' – 7 June 1954 – he took his life with a cyanide-dipped apple.

'Should do well,' had been as far as his old schoolmaster Sherborne, problem- and puzzle-setter Canon D.B. Eperson, said about Turing's prospects when he was a youth:

*He thought rapidly, even brilliantly, and was seldom defeated by a problem, but his methods were often crude, cumbersome and untidy. He showed no interest in school games, music making, or in the activities of the school archaeological society and the gramophone society that I organised. He answered my puzzles but through his own alternative methods.*

Sherborne School featured in a spy scare on the outbreak of war in 1939. In the school's official history it is noted that it gave refuge to 'Jews and Germans' and that 'one was afterwards for a time interned'. He was identified for the author in 1971 by Victor Swatridge, the Aliens Officer at police divisional headquarters in Sherborne, from 1934:

*I had to register a man of magnificent physique, a young blonde Prussian named Heinz Brack. Brack was a most charming man and regarded as a delightful person by his associates at the school. He quite often paid visits, under any pretext, to the divisional office, which aroused my suspicions, and when I refused the information he required, became arrogant and demanding. Discreetly and unobtrusively I introduced the name of Heinz Brack into the conversation when dealing with new female arrivals and those returning to their homeland. On mentioning the name, there was a distinct change of attitude which carried with it a frightening expression on the faces of aliens. I intensified my enquiries and found that Brack was away from his lodgings every weekend, travelling extensively in the south-western counties. I was confident that he was busily engaged in subversion and had a great influence and control of German nationals in this area, possibly part of an espionage network.*

A year later the war visited the town on a warm but cloudy Monday afternoon. It was at 15.55 hours on 30 September 1940 that Yeovil's barrage balloons were raised and the air-raid sirens also wailed in nearby Sherborne. Above the Somerset town, 37 Heinkel He.111 bombers were trying to find the Westland Aircraft Company's works and aerodrome but nine-tenths cloud cover at 20,000 feet made this an impossible task.

Instead, flying in formation on a north-easterly line that had been set from glimpses of the railway line, they missed their target by five miles. The drone of bombers passed harmlessly over Yeovil and they approached Sherborne from the western sky. Shortly after four o'clock they began to bomb blind in the vicinity of Lenthay Common and continued across central Sherborne, raining down some 100 bombs – the number is still disputed – on the clustered terraces between scholastic and ecclesiastical roofs. The raid lasted about four minutes. Littleton Powys was living in a bungalow in Priestlands:

*I remember that it seemed to me there was an earthquake for it was impossible to distinguish the fall of a single bomb. Then the ceiling of the bathroom fell upon my head, and suddenly I heard Mabel saying quite coolly, 'It's all right, Mrs Griffiths, never mind, it is all over now, Mrs Griffiths,' but the earth, for all her words of consolation, was still quaking. Poor Mrs Griffiths had been coming to us to measure some curtains; she was trying to find our house, and, while doing so, the bombs began to fall; she rushed into the nearest house, which happened to be ours, and as was to be expected after such an experience, she was pale as death.*

Fortunately the population was relatively dispersed as the schoolchildren had just gone home. Amazingly, with bombs falling all around, the famous Abbey and its surrounding complex of ancient buildings escaped almost unscathed. Most of the bombs fell on homes, roads and shops. Of the town's 1,700 buildings, 86 were destroyed or ruined, and another 680 required repairs. Mostly this was to rectify blast damage to windows and roofs of buildings such as the Big School which otherwise survived with their fittings unscathed. Electricity and telephone lines were disconnected, gas and water mains cut, and sewers fractured. Even in the relative warmth of late summer there was considerable distress and the Red Cross had to bring in blankets.

In all 18 people were killed, including one who was critically wounded, and another 31 casualties were taken to hospital. The names of those who died are recorded beside the War Memorial in the Abbey precinct in Half Moon Street:

| | |
|---|---|
| John Butlin | Albert I.E. le Gallais |
| Leonard Dawe | Arthur J. Lintern |
| Albertina B. Gartell | Elizabeth A. Marden |
| Percy H.D. Goulter | William S. Morgan |
| Douglas Hunt | A.H. Reason |
| Henry Ireland | Barry A. Trask |
| William C. Jeffery | Patricia A. Warren |
| Edward D. Knobbs | Robert K. Warren |
| Horace G. Legg | Ronald G. Warren |

The heroine among the debris was Miss Maud Steele, supervisor of the telephone exchange, which was blown apart by a direct hit. She ensured that casualty reports were relayed by road. For her bravery she was awarded the George Cross which had been instituted by King George VI – as 'the Civilians VC' – only a few days earlier.

Hurricanes were in action around Sherborne from the surrounding counties but Dorset's Front-Line fighter was the Spitfire from RAF Warmwell in the gravel fields east of Dorchester. There Squadron Leader Peter Devitt could muster only eight, and of these some 'should not have flown by peacetime standards'. He was ordered by Middle Wallop sector control to scramble and proceed as quickly as possible to Yeovil. There he had the same problem as the German bombers – too much cloud – and failed to find them:

*Thinking that perhaps they had delivered their bombs and swung round through 180 degrees to starboard as they had done on a previous Bristol raid, I turned the squadron eastwards in the hope of picking them up. They had obviously turned this way so as not to be silhouetted against a background of white cloud for our fighters to pick up. It is always more difficult to pick up a camouflaged aircraft from above and with the earth below, but a fighter must have the advantage of height in order to deliver his full weight in the first attack.*

*A few seconds after I had spotted them I saw their bombs falling away from beneath their bellies. On looking down to see what the target was, to my horror I saw the old school Courts which I knew so well* [as a Sherborne School pupil, 1924–29]. *I was at the time just in a position to attack, which I did but was molested by a pack of Bf.109s which I had not noticed sitting above the Heinkels, and above me as well. I could not see much of where the bombs fell as I was too intent on what was going on around me. I did, however, see in one instant a great deal of smoke around the old buildings and so knew there must be some hits and damage and probably casualties.*

Another briefly engaging in the formation, 19-year-old Pilot Officer Eric 'Boy' Marrs (so called for his youthful looks), limped back to Warmwell in a crippled Spitfire and found only one of his wheels would come down. It would not then retract, and to attempt a landing on one wheel is much more hazardous than a belly flop. Marrs turned off the engine and glided in to land, touching down on the grass as gently as possible:

*I began to slew round and counteracted as much as possible with the brake on the wheel which was down. I ended up going sideways on one wheel, a tail wheel, and a wing tip. Luckily the good tyre held out and the only damage to the aeroplane, apart from that done by the bullets, is a wing tip which is easily replaceable. I hopped out and went to the Medical Officer to get a lot of splinters picked out of my leg and wrist. I felt jolly glad to be down on the ground without having caught fire.*

Sergeant Pilot Leslie Arthur Edwin Reddington, in Spitfire L1072 of 152 Squadron, ran out of luck on 30 September 1940. He was shot down into the sea off Portland. The 26-year-old was from Coventry where his wife was pregnant with their daughter who was named Lesley, in his memory, on her birth in February 1941.

Hurricanes of 56 Squadron from RAF Boscombe Down, Wiltshire, also had an eventful day. They came off worse in the dogfights, losing half their aircraft in crashes across Dorset, though all the pilots were able to bale out or force-land safely.

I have been collecting these details of Dorset's war since I became a newspaper reporter in 1964. In 1984 I interviewed Edward J. Freeman, wartime District Air Raid Precautions Controller, who had been Clerk to Sherborne Urban District Council from 1936 until its abolition in 1974. He had retired to a bungalow at Rimpton and was keen that his memories should be recorded. All his basic facts can be corroborated but the passage of time led to a degree of exaggeration:

*The Sherborne raid is being forgotten. Last year I heard a guide at Sherborne Castle say in answer to a question, about whether any bombs had fallen at Sherborne during the war, that he thought there had been one dropped in the town. I interrupted to say that I had*

*been the town's ARP controller and there had been 300 bombs* [though perhaps there was only a third of that number, with some reducing the figure to 60] *that fell in three minutes on 30 September 1940.*

*At the time I was on the pavement in Yeovil standing in a queue to see a picture – it was one of the few days in the entire war when I was away from my desk. It was my birthday. The thud of the bombs in the east was followed by a pall of black smoke, which could only be from Sherborne, and I drove straight back. It took me 20 minutes to reach the council offices, picking my way through an unimaginable shambles.*

*The theory is that the 50 German planes had been on their way to the Bristol Aeroplane Company works at Filton* [seriously damaged by an attack five days earlier, on 25 September, though in fact the attack was against Westlands at Yeovil] *and were intercepted by a squadron of Hurricanes, two of which were brought down each side of Yeovil. The local people thought one of the pilots was German as they saw his parachute open. The bombers came to us from the south-west, across Lenthay Common, and then they unloaded. We were underneath.*

*There were no longer any services at all. No water, no telephones – the exchange had a direct hit – no gas, no electricity, and the sewers and all roads out of the town were blocked.*

*One of the miracles was in Newland where Foster's Infants School received a direct hit and had to be pulled down afterwards. It was hit only a quarter of an hour after the children had left. One story I heard, though I cannot vouch for it, was that in the Avenue, Miss Billinger climbed from her bath into the open air* [Miss Margaret Billinger lived at Stonegarth]. *Perhaps the strangest damage was in Horsecastles where bombs landed on both sides of the terrace and then outhouses imploded away from the main buildings, which was caused by a bellows effect. Six or eight delayed action bombs went off 12 hours later. One caught us out as it was hidden under debris.*

*The strangest debris came from the midnight bakery next to the Picture Palace in Newland. They had hoarded silver coins which were thrown on to the cinema roof and retrieved by my ARP warden. As I plotted the bombs on to our ARP area map and the number climbed into the hundreds I ran out of red pins. It was quite extraordinary that there hadn't been more casualties.*

*The worst thing was a direct hit in the cemetery. The coffin of a friend whom we had buried a week earlier was blown out of the ground. My gravediggers disappeared and we did the best we could to clear up with a firm of undertakers from Yeovil.*

*Down Lenthay there was terrible damage and I sent the Billeting Officer down on his bike to see how many I had to rehouse and find accommodation for. Ten of our council houses were completely destroyed, and there was damage to all the remaining 108 of them, mainly on a serious scale. To my astonishment when he came back he said: 'No need to worry – people have come forward* and offered shelter. Everyone has been given a home somewhere.' It was quite extraordinary what happened there, and it happened all over the town. If ever I have admired the people of Sherborne as a whole it was after the raid. I had told the schools that they might have to put people up that night, but in the event it wasn't necessary. One little thing, after that raid there was no all-clear, as we had no electricity. From then on we had to use rattles and whistles for air-raid sirens.

The ministry men thought I was exaggerating and panicking when they heard from me on the only emergency phone line we had left, but when they came down they apologised to me. They had never seen such devastation in a small country town. I took the Regional Commissioner around in my car. Twelve hours later all my tyres were flat, punctured by the glass.

Opposite Phillips and Son's store, outside the Westminster Bank [junction of Half Moon Street and South Street], an unexploded bomb had fallen, leaving a hole that the bomb disposal team had covered with sandbags. An officer calmly sat there beside these on a lump of stone and lit a cigarette. I showed some concern that we were sitting beside a bomb. 'If it goes off, we won't know anything about it!,' he said. 'It's a big one,' he said, 'but I can't reach it for a fortnight. In the meantime you'll have to evacuate everyone around.' The police and Army sealed off the area, and we got the stretcher cases out as best we could. [For the next two weeks east–west movements through the town were through the Courts of Sherborne School.] I had to arrange temporary rationing arrangements because we couldn't get into the butcher's shop [that of Charles Greenham]. A fortnight later that officer came back to me laughing, saying: 'You'll never believe me, Mr Freeman, but it was only a small one. The big hole was because it had gone down a disused well-shaft!'

I was flooded with visits from people in London, Bristol, Reading and the cities, and had to explain how we got out of difficulties. It is surprising how the help came that we needed – there was a wonderful spirit everywhere. The ministry admitted that there were certain things we had to do that might be outside the law, but they said go ahead anyway as legislation was on its way.

I still wonder how the devil we coped as well with it all. Twenty or thirty evacuees would come down the day after a London raid and we would have to find homes for them. The evacuation was worked out on paper and by the train timetables, but we would have cases where 600 would come down from one school, bound for Sherborne, and some of ours would get off at Sidmouth. We had to sort all that out, have the doctors inspect them, and give out 48-hour rations. You saw how people had been living in London. It was a trying time, particularly as my staff were being called up. We coped by making our minds up at a moment's notice.

One night I had a red warning that there would be a raid, and suddenly the whole place was lit up by parachute flares, but then nothing happened. We had

Above: *Realistic casualty with a detached eye – courtesy the butcher – taking part in Exercise Demon in Newland in May 1943.*

been told that if the flares dropped they would be followed by bombs. The lights ringed the town and someone phoned to say there was a landmine hanging over his front door, but it was a flare that had caught in his chimney. He was so excited and frightened he said he couldn't get out of the house – I asked him what had happened to the back door.

I kept on good terms with most of the town. The only time I upset the school [Sherborne School] was when I requisitioned its tuck shop as a British Restaurant. Later in the war, because of our experiences, we were chosen for bomb instruction exercises, and a special invasion exercise in Newland in May 1943. For that one they had a particularly realistic casualty, with his eye hanging by a thread, provided by a butcher. I think they went too far. One old lady in the crowd fainted.

My biggest regret is that I didn't keep a diary, but I never had the time. A little regret is that there was a relic that could have been preserved, three pieces of bomb-case that were embedded out of harm's way in a school wall [at Sherborne School] I asked General Waller, the bursar, to leave them but he had them hooked out and the stone repaired.

Brigadier-General Richard Lancelot Waller (1875–1961), a veteran of the Boer War and the First World War, retired to Lindum House in Lenthay Road. He was the bursar of Sherborne School from 1931 to 1945. His last military post, in 1931, had been Chief Engineer at Southern Command; it was asking a bit much for him to appreciate the aesthetics of shrapnel.

Sherborne's highest ranking officer of the Second World War, commander of the Eighth Army in Italy, was General Sir Richard Loudon McCreery (1898–1967) who is buried in Sherborne cemetery in Lenthay Road. He won the Military Cross on the Western Front in the First World War, commanded an armoured-car regiment between the wars, and was awarded the Distinguished Service Order when the British Army returned to France in 1940.

As Major-General he was Chief of Staff Middle East in 1942, was knighted in 1943, and went with the

Eighth Army from Sicily to Italy, being promoted Lieutenant-General and becoming their commander from 1944 until the end of the war. In the immediate postwar period he commanded the British Army of Occupation in Austria.

Back in Dorset, Sherborne Silk Mill – which had been taken over by Frederick Marsden from Coventry in 1937 – had been turned into a pioneering centre for the manufacture of 'substitutes for silk'. The company had been making black silk scarves for sailors – already replaced by rayon – but it was in more profound applications that 'a new wonder material' had potential. This was glass-fibre fabric, in 36-inch-wide sheets of 2mm thickness, which was developed in September 1942 as a refinement of weavable glass yarn that had been invented by the Owens Corning Fibreglas Corporation of New York and Toledo, Ohio, in 1939.

Its immediate wartime use was for electrical insulation tape. Far from being merely a substitute for silk, it was found to be a considerable advancement, with softening and eventual melting being delayed until temperatures exceeded 700 degrees Centigrade. This enabled the doubling of output power from small motors. The material was also ideal for diaphragms of respirators. Once again it offered advantages, above existing products, in that it did not deteriorate with age or break down under bacteriological attack. Marsden's first specialist customer was the Chemical Defence Experimental Station at Porton Down.

Marsden's Glass was registered under the tradename Marglass during the winter of 1942. By the summer of 1943 the works was re-configured to concentrate on its production. Output to the 2mm specification had reached 3,000 square yards a week and was continuing to rise. Even after the end of the war in Europe, some of the applications of the product and even the location of the factory – 'a silk mill in this country' – remained covered by censorship.

Wartime visitors included the actor James Cagney who entertained patients at the United States Field Hospital in Haydon Park and Lance-Bombadier Harry Secombe, who was stationed at Crendle Court, Milborne Port. The latter appeared in the Church Hall in Digby Road.

Revelations that came to light in 1997 as a result of the American Freedom of Information Act show that an 'enemy agents' story was invented as a cover-up to conceal the fact that a combat exercise course had been laid out in Sherborne Park within the confines of the 228th Field Hospital Unit of the United States Army. That meant the site of a massive explosion, at midday on Monday 20 March 1944, came under the auspices and protection of the International Red Cross under the terms of the Geneva Convention and should not have been used by armed personnel, nor for the storing of ammunition, let alone for the laying of a live minefield.

The colossal bang took place 500 yards east-south-east of Sherborne Castle, 50 yards on the Haydon side of Castleton public footpath number 6 which runs from Home Farm to The Camp on the south side of Sherborne Park (ST 650 159).

'It was a tremendous explosion, the loudest anyone had ever heard,' said 16-year-old Tod Frost who was threshing a corn rick beside the private road in front of Sherborne Castle and had a Land Army girl hurled on top of him in the straw, being almost impaled on her pitchfork. 'Bits of lorry and bodies were strewn across half a mile,' he continued. One truck had totally disintegrated and others were mangled. Troops and ambulances from the nearby camp came to clear up but later 'open lorries passed along the road directly beneath us. We could see the rows of mutilated bodies covered with ground-sheets. It was an appaling sight.'

The number of casualties was variously given as 29 (now listed on the commemorative plaque in Half Moon Street); 35 to 40; and up to 140. Betty Warner, then aged 23 and living in Coombe, on the other side of the town, writes that 'the whole of Sherborne heard the explosion' and records in her diary a death-toll of 37, including her new-found friends Joseph B. Henning and Lucien P. Pessoz: 'Another American, Frank, came to tell us Joe and Lucien had been killed with 35 others.' All accounts agree that there were only bodies to be counted and no injured to be tended.

The accident happened when a lorry slipped back onto a mine during clearing up after an exercise with anti-tank and anti-personnel mines by the United States 294th Combat Engineer Company. The wheels came to rest on an 8lb anti-tank mine, the bellows of which would have needed a pressure of 250lbs to trigger detonation. That set off all the mines stacked in the truck. What happened next was that a myth was spun. On realising the embarrassing illegality of the incident, because of the abuse of hospital camp status, a cover story was invented. Sherborne Park, it was said, had been infiltrated by German agents who brought a truckload of mines into an Army physical training course, with the culprits being named as Kurt Henlein and Ernst Buchner, who would be executed at Salisbury, by the military, in May 1944.

Censorship and news management was the norm. Such manipulation was vital to avoid giving indications to the enemy of the size and disposition of the American Army – by this time 80,000 strong in the Dorset area – that had built up on the coast opposite the Cherbourg peninsula and Normandy beaches. Secrecy and security became a convenient cloak for incompetence. Dorset's Americans went on to take Omaha Beach where their official casualty list – including some lost in previous accidents – were 2,811 killed, 5,744 missing or taken prisoner, and 13,546 seriously injured.

One of the war's most glorious failures accompanied the attempt to take the famous 'Bridge too far'.

Envisaged as a bold venture to move the war forward – despite intercepted Enigma-decoded communications indicating they were landing beside recuperating Front-Line troops from the Russian front – British airborne landings at Arnhem became an exercise in over-confidence. Lieutenant John Grayburn of the Oxfordshire and Buckinghamshire Light Infantry was an old Shirburnian. Attached as a platoon commander to the 2nd Battalion, the Parachute Regiment, under Colonel John Dutton Frost, he was tasked to 'take and hold' the great steel bridge over the Lower Rhine in three days of gallant fighting between 17–20 September 1944.

After the northern end had been captured, Grayburn was ordered forward, to seize the southern end. Repeated attempts were made until the rate of casualties made progress impossible. Grayburn directed the withdrawal of his men 'into comparative cover' and gave them cover from an exposed embankment. He was the last man to come off the bridge. Then his platoon occupied a house in an almost indefensible position and held off sustained attacks by German infantry, mortars, tanks and self-propelled guns. John Grayburn continued to lead his men: 'He constantly exposed himself to the enemy's fire while moving among and encouraging his platoon and seemed completely oblivious to danger.'

Then, forced out of the house on 19 September, Grayburn carried out an audacious return to the bridge, with a fighting patrol, to prevent the Germans from laying demolition charges. Then, though wounded in the back and without having eaten for days, he pulled back to another untenable position. Here, in full view of a German tank, Grayburn directed his men back to relative safety and stayed on the Front-Line, where he was killed on the night of 20 September. His citation for the award of the Victoria Cross concludes: 'There is no doubt that had it not been for this officer's inspiring bravery, the Arnhem bridge could never have been held for this time.'

The roll of honour, published in *The Shirburnian* during the Second World War, totalled 242 names. This is compared with 218 in the First World War but the school was then only half the size. Lieutenant John Grayburn's posthumous Victoria Cross, the first to be won for the Parachute Regiment, was the only one awarded to a Shirburnian in this war.

Sherborne School made its debut in film in 1948, completing the trio of a book, play and a movie, as the setting for *The Guinea-Pig* by old Shirburnian playwright Warren Chetham-Strode (1896–1974).

*Below and right: Bomb-damaged houses towards the eastern end of Newland providing an authentic setting for Exercise Demon on 9 May 1943; cottage clearances* (left) *and the removal of the remaining walls of No. 88 Newland* (far right) *have changed the scene, but No. 100* (centre), *No. 92 and No. 90* (right) *survive, in a view south-eastwards in 1984.*

# Second World War

Left: *Civilians killed in the Sherborne Blitz on 30 September 1940, listed beside the town's War Memorial in Half Moon Street.*

Bottom: *The Women's Voluntary Service van arrives* (right) *with tea urns for street fighters and stretcher-bearers* (left) *taking part in Exercise Demon, seen in a view eastwards down Newland on 9 May 1943.*

Below: *Newland Flats* (left) *and the surrounding lawn and paths have replaced bomb-damaged buildings on the north side of Newland, though the seventeenth-century house with mullioned windows* (centre right) *remains, as pictured in 1984.*

Below: *German troops, looking like the real thing in captured uniforms though they spoke broad Dorset, rounded up in Newland after street-fighting for Exercise Demon in May 1943.*

Above: *The last surviving Nissen hut of wartime Haydon Camp.*

Right: *Wartime water-tower, which supplied Haydon Camp, in the woods on Jerusalem Hill.*

Left: *Explosion site, in the middle of this field near Sherborne Castle, where a company of 29 United States Engineers were blown up by their own mines on 20 March 1944.*

*Memorial to the men of the 294th Engineer Combat Battalion of the United States Army killed beside Sherborne Park.*

Left: *Children at Foster's Infants School in Newland had just gone home when the Luftwaffe visited Sherborne on 30 September 1940.*

Right: *Foster's Infants School stood beside Tinney's Lane (centre) and has been replaced by Nos 1 to 6 Newland Flats (right), seen in a view north-westwards in 1984.*

Left: *Replacement Green Bushes (left), restored Tanglin (centre) and repaired Pentire (right) in a view south-eastwards from North Road in 1984.*

Right: *Semi-detached Green Bushes (left) and Tanglin (centre) in North Road, owned by builder Thomas Penny, were reduced to half a house on 30 September 1940, with roof damage to Pentire (far right).*

Left: *The back of Mrs D. Robertson's Homemead, on the west side of Acreman Street, looking east towards the town from a garden covered with debris below an unscathed monkey-puzzle tree on 1 October 1940.*

Below: *The Knapp on the west side of Acreman Street, seen from the south-east, was left as a gap between cottages and terraced houses by a direct hit from a German bomb on 30 September 1940.*

Above: *Ashbourne and its flat-roofed balcony extension* (left), *with Stonecroft next door* (right), *seen from the south-west, in Richmond Road on 1 October 1940.*

Right: *The Sherborne Urban District Council's housing estate in Lenthay Road received Sherborne's first bombs as the formation of German bombers approached from Yeovil on the afternoon of 30 September 1940.*

Below: *Detail of roof damage to council-owned houses in Lenthay Road, Sherborne, which would be rebuilt to the same design.*

*Partially cleared, with props just about supporting the remains of Phillips and Son's outfitting department (left), and the public bar of the Half Moon Hotel (right), seen from the north-west in October 1940.*

Left: *The day after Sherborne was blitzed, from the bottom end of Cheap Street, south-westwards along Half Moon Street to the Half Moon Hotel (centre).*

Below: *Crater at the bottom of Cheap Street, looking eastwards from Half Moon Street and the debris of Phillips and Son's (right) to the shops of butcher Charles Greenham and shoe retailer Joseph Frisby on 1 October 1940.*

Bottom left: *Westwards along Half Moon Street from the junction with Cheap Street, on 1 October 1940, to the shops in ancient Church House (right).*

*Sedber in the Avenue, rebuilt and renamed Rathgar, from the north-west, 1984.*

Left: *Stonegarth in Newland was held together by its chimney on 30 September 1940, enabling Miss Margaret Billinger to survive the blast as she was taking her afternoon bath.*

Above: *Sedber, on the east side of the Avenue, seen from the north-west on 1 October 1940.*

Left: *The centre of Cheap Street in a view southwards to T.E. Gillard's hairdressing salon beside the path leading to the Methodist Church, with the sign above the clearance team on 1 October 1940 reading 'Have Faith in God'.*

Below: *The remains of Stonegarth were demolished but replacement stone-built houses incorporate oak lintels and a medieval slit window (centre gable), seen in a view north-westwards from Newland, across Tinney's Lane to the Avenue in 1984.*

## Twenty-One

### ❖
# *1950–1959*

Sir Hubert Medlycott, chairman of Sherborne School governors, chatted to Queen Elizabeth as the assistant master, Major John David Buchanan of the Grenadier Guards, presented a guard of honour for inspection by King George VI on Thursday 1 June 1950.

From 1947 until 1954 the high-speed Devon Belle express of Pullman carriages swept through Sherborne on the summertime service from Waterloo to Ilfracombe. It was one of the last gasps of lost style from the Southern Railway as it became a mere region of newly nationalised British Railways. Among the Pacific Battle of Britain class locomotives hauling the de-luxe carriages was No. 34051 *Winston Churchill* which eventually took his namesake from London to his grave.

The town's 'Black Friday' deluge took place on 15 August 1952. Three inches of rain fell in as many hours and turned Cheap Street and Greenhill into rivers. Flash-floods inundated lower-lying parts of the towns from Newell and Westbury to Long Street and Castleton.

The War Memorial extension to the Big School building at Sherborne School was declared open by Brigadier Charles Edward Hudson VC at noon on Saturday 10 November 1956.

Daily operations at Marglass Limited were taken over by Peter Marsden from his father Frederick. They decided to take the main part of the business out of Sherborne Silk Mill in Ottery Road and return it to the former Westbury Mill site on the opposite side of the junction, around an arm of the River Yeo. Here, after doing a deal with builder W.J. Spiller, there was room for a factory, built in 1956, north-east of the railway bridge. More looms were installed and the fabric-finishing shed extended eastwards, in 1960, after the river had been re-routed to the south side of the railway. Advancements brought about by the international space race created new demands for thermoset resins in printed circuit boards for transistors, followed by silicon chip microprocessors, keeping glass fabrics at the heart of electronic technology. The older buildings of Westbury Mill were retained as maintenance facilities and workshops.

In 1959 the Sherborne School Cadet Force was inspected by Field-Marshal Viscount Montgomery of Alamein following his retirement as Deputy Supreme Commander of Nato. It was called a 'saluting the colour' ceremony though technically it was a drill banner as only military units are allowed to have a flag that is consecrated and saluted. Wearing a peaked cap rather than his familiar Tank Corps' beret, Monty presented the new standard to Regimental Sergeant Major Venning. Someone mentioned that the nation's most famous living soldier would now have more time for such occasions. 'Field-Marshals remain on the active list for life,' the sprightly 71-year-old replied.

*Luxury Pullman coaches of the Devon Belle, hauled by Battle of Britain class locomotive No. 34051 Winston Churchill, passing the Old Castle on an express summertime service between 1947 and 1954.*

*Sherborne Station, with buildings from 1860 (top left), looking eastwards along the up-platform (left).*

# Railway

*Down-platform (right), in a view westwards, at Sherborne Station.*

Above: *Castleton village and the Old Castle (top right) from the bridge carrying New Road over the railway.*

Centre right: *Steps and footbridge from the down-platform at Sherborne.*

Right: *'Stop, look and listen' when using the public path that crosses the railway at Wyke.*

Below left: *The line from Castleton into Sherborne (top right).*

Main: *Passing Wyke Barns, en route to Waterloo.*

# Twenty-Two

❧

# *1960–1969*

Marglass Limited was taken over, from its founding Marsden family, in a joint venture by Courtaulds and United Merchants and Manufacturers in 1962.

Sherborne Cadet Corps trooped its colour before Earl Mountbatten of Burma in 1963. Monday 17 June that year saw the death of the scion of the literary Powys clan in Blaenau-Ffestiniog at the age of 90. Though born at Shirley in Derbyshire, and having died in the 'Land of his Fathers' – he traced his descent from the Welsh princes – John Cowper Powys wanted his ashes cast upon the Dorset sea. That was done, from the Chesil Beach at Abbotsbury – because he had used the treacherous shingle bank for the shipwreck scene in his novel *Weymouth Sands* (1934). There, Angus Wilson considered, he wrote 'not of heroes or even of men, but of men beside nature.' Of *Wolf Solent* the *Sunday Times* had written in 1929: 'Its background is Dorset, and it is a Dorset which has rarely been painted more graciously, even by Hardy himself.'

The country of *Wolf Solent* is from the Powys public schooldays at Sherborne, westwards across the pasture and former pond of Lenthay Common to Bradford Abbas, and to the big cities of this world – Yeovil, Dorchester and Weymouth.

It was a case of absence making the mind pound faster as he travelled the United States – missing only two in its contemporary pre-Hawaii and Alaska boundaries – and his was a more hedonistic philosophy than that of his author brothers.

Among his other novels are *Wood* and *Stone* and the period piece *The Brazen Head*. Poetry included *Wolfsbane*, *Mandragora* and *Samphire*, and the deeper thoughts are in *The Religion of a Sceptic* and *In Defence of Sensuality*. His literary criticism, on which he lectured in the States, ranged from *Visions and Revisions* and *The Meaning of Culture* in 1930 to his 1934 autobiography, *Morwyn*, in 1937 and *The Pleasures of Literature* in 1938.

Robert Powell (1904–98) was the headmaster of Sherborne School from 1950 to 1970. He appointed talented history masters who balanced what had been a reputation for excellence on the rugby field with its best-ever Oxbridge entrance successes in 1959. Shirburnians scooped 21 awards and beat all the competition apart from Manchester Grammar School. Throughout the 1960s, Powell held out against the 'creeping liberalism' that threatened cherished institutions and their traditional practices from cold baths and corporal punishment to fagging and learning Latin.

Dining with Monica Hutchings and myself, in the winter of 1969, he recounted anecdotes of how MGM had 'stitched-up the school by providing Coca Cola rather than cash' for its use as the setting for a remake of the classic film *Goodbye Mr Chips*. Its new stars were Peter O'Toole and Petula Clarke. Powell showed more interest in 'the new science labs', completed in 1966, beside West Lodge and Acreman Street, which were named the Alan Turing Laboratories in honour of the dishevelled mathematical genius who invented the first programmed digital computer in the world and deciphered the German Enigma codes during the Second World War.

*Sherborne Gas Works (left) before the arrival of piped supplies from the North Sea in the 1970s.*

*Sculptures in the art room at Sherborne School.*

# *Castleton*

Top: *Edwardian Castleton, looking eastwards to St Mary Magdalen Church* (left) *and closed gates at the entrance to the Old Castle.*

Above left: *Castleton* (left) *and the Old Castle* (central skyline), *eastwards from New Road, which has replaced the former highway south from the village* (far right).

Above: *Dinney Bridge carried the medieval road southwards from Castleton.*

Left: *Underneath Dinney Bridge, from the River Yeo, showing a combination of medieval and Tudor arches.*

Left: *Now owned by Wessex Water, the 26-foot diameter overshoot water-wheel inside these buildings used to power three vertical rams but is now regarded as industrial archaeology.*

Below: *Castleton Water Works with its 1868-built classical Pump House.*

Below left: *High-level inlet to the Water Works from the River Yeo* (top left) *and its outlet leat* (foreground).

Below right: *St Mary's Church was rebuilt on its present site in Castleton village by Sir Walter Raleigh in 1601.*

Ralegh House, Middle House and Lattice House – reputedly the most haunted in Sherborne – forming the post-medieval terrace that is all that is left of the former main street beside the perimeter drive into the Old Castle precinct.

Thatched Turnpike Cottage, beside Castle Farm, takes its name from Doghouse Lane Gate.

Here lieth ȳ Body of MARGARET BARNARD An old faithful Servant to ȳ Earls of Bristol And their Succeſsors above Seventy years She gave twenty pounds towards ȳ building of this Church and departed this Life April the tenth An: Dom: 1716 Aged 96

Centre right: Pride of place in St Mary's Church goes to this memorial over a door, to 96-year-old Margaret Barnard, 'faithful servant to ye Earls of Bristol' who died in 1716.

Right: Thirsk Lodge and the Firs, a grand Victorian edge-of-town villa overlooking Oborne Road, which is now a peg down in the world and divided into two.

# Twenty-Three

# *1970–1979*

Britain's worst ever hospital disaster occurred at Coldharbour Hospital (ST 643 175) at 02.55 hours on 5 July 1972 when flames swept through its Winfrith Ward. Some 30 severely mentally subnormal patients died. They were aged from 14 to 49 and had relatives or guardians mostly in Dorset and Hampshire. Evacuation of the victims was particularly difficult and harrowing because of their mental condition. Only six from the ward were saved.

Winfrith Ward had been refurbished, in an £85,000 facelift, only six weeks before. This modernisation contributed to the death-toll. A false ceiling, which had been intended to make the former RAF barracks 'more cosy', produced a horizontal chimney for the 96-foot building. An inquiry also listed other shortcomings which led to a thorough revision of safety guidelines throughout the land. Furnishings were combustible; some of them being highly flammable. There were no smoke detectors. Two fire-escape doors were locked. Evidence was produced of smoking by staff whilst on duty.

The single male nurse in attendance that night, 31-year-old Fred Rawles, was exonerated for his inability to evacuate all the patients. He had no chance to react in time, the findings revealed, because the flames were funnelled along the ceiling cavity at a tremendous speed. This was estimated to have been between 50 and 60 miles an hour. The fire was followed by a fundamental change of Government policy, towards care in the community, and by the end of the century the site of Coldharbour Hospital was covered by the new suburbia of Granville Way and Albany Close.

Land used for Sherborne's annual sheep fair, in Hound Street, was given to Sherborne Urban District Council by Simon Wingfield-Digby, MP. It was earmarked for the new Digby Hall, which opened in April 1972, and a replacement Sherborne Library, which followed in July 1972. The previous home for the library, since 1949, had been in the Julian in Higher Cheap Street. The move, into 4,266 square feet of floor space, enabled the doubling of the

*The Conduit and commerce keeping up custom and tradition at the heart of the town.*

lending library stock to 12,000 adult books, plus 2,200 titles for children, and 2,000 for reference purposes. Fred Pitfield designed the new building for Dorset County Council and it was built by A.O. Cutler Limited from Shaftesbury.

The decade also saw changes in the landscape for Sherborne Park. Having been maturing for over two centuries, its lake was silting and shrinking, as sedge-beds encroached. Decisive action was taken in 1973 when temporary ponds were created on the south side of Sherborne Castle so that a 'Mud Cat', operated by G.L, Manthorp Limited, from Marlow, could be floated onto the remaining water to cut into the sediment. As a result the average depth was increased from 2 feet to 12 feet and its capacity by tenfold, to 120 million gallons. Its overflow outlet, built in 1973, takes the pressure off the picturesque Cascade.

Boys from Sherborne School adopted the town's last surviving water-mill in 1975. West Mill Restoration Society worked for the rest of the decade to rescue the building on the River Yeo at the far end of West Mill Lane (ST 633 154). Mark Hinton, the society's 16-year-old chairman, described it as being 'in a horrible state of dereliction'. One wall was missing and the roof had gone. On the other hand, not only was the water-wheel intact, but the driving mechanism was also still in harness.

The site, beside the sewage works, still retains a great deal of character. It lies at the foot of an escarpment below Honeycombe Wood. In clearing out mud from the former mill leat, the boys found the remains of a leather packhorse saddle, and a seed merchant's cart. People from the town came forward with a collection of other relics that had been salvaged from the other half-dozen former mills in and around Sherborne. Success was proclaimed when the 12-foot-diameter cast-iron wheel turned again for the first time since the Second World War. West Mill, a Grade II listed building, probably dates from 1720 to 1750. An Elizabethan map in Sherborne Museum indicates an earlier mill on the same site and traces of its foundations were discovered during the project.

Words of encouragement came from old Shirburnian Hugh Swynnerton Thomas, 1st Baron Thomas (born 1932) who went on from Sherborne to Cambridge and the Sorbonne. He emerged during the Cold War as a campaigner for nuclear disarmament and a student of revolution and conflict, with studies such as *The Spanish Civil War*, in 1981, and the brilliantly conceived *Unfinished History of the World*, in 1979. As with West Mill, the historian had a good decade, and was rewarded with a life peerage in 1981.

Despite personal best efforts at keeping it going, the Greenhill Bookshop on the Green closed in 1973, and our trade transferred downhill to Nigel Coldwell's Abbey Bookshop in the Parade. Here his aunt was in perpetual motion along the shelves, sighing as she turned each title so that the words on the spine read upwards (old style) rather than downwards (new style). As a result, browsers found every word was upside down, and it passed several pleasurable minutes taking out books at random and turning them the other way around as the indomitable lady shadowed our progress.

Old Shirburnian and England cricketer David Sheppard (born 1929), who played for his country 22 times between 1950 to 1963 and captained the team in 1954, was appointed Bishop of Liverpool in 1975.

The Right Revd John Dudley Galtrey Kirkham (born 1935) was appointed Bishop Suffragan of Sherborne in 1976, as he wrote to remind me from Little Bailie, Sturminster Marshall, after I had rashly written that 'there is no longer a Bishop of Sherborne'. The Archdeacon of Sherborne, the Ven. Edwin James Greenfield Ward (born 1919), rector of West Stafford and former chaplain to Queen Elizabeth II, took up his appointment in 1967. The secular Sherborne title, created in 1784, was previously held by Charles Dutton, 7th Baron Sherborne (1911–82) who lived at Aldsworth, near Cheltenham.

Above: *Gnome-seller and wares pitched on the pavement of the Parade, opposite Lloyd's Bank* (top left), *in 1972.*

Below: *Cheap Street policed* (left) *and Pack Monday Fair stalls around the Conduit* (centre) *in 1972.*

# Twenty-Four

❖

# *1980–1989*

Marglass Ltd, owned by Courtaulds and United Merchants, received a £2,250,000 rejuvenation in 1980 with the installation of 100 high-speed shuttle-less looms. Annual sales had reached £12 million.

Sherborne School cadet Alex Dewhurst won the British paragliding distance record in 1980 when he was released from behind a Land Rover at 780 feet on Batcombe Down and was airborne for 3.75km across the Blackmore Vale.

The Sherborne barony passed to an elder cousin, Ralph Stawell Dutton, 8th Baron Sherborne (1898–1985) on the death of the 7th Baron on Christmas Day in 1982. A prolific writer on the English country house and its gardens, the 8th Baron lived at Hinton Ampner, near Alresford, Hampshire. He had served on the Historic Buildings Council and committees of the National Trust and was a trustee of the Wallace Collection of fine art. He had no heir, however, and the Sherborne title from 1784 was declared extinct at his death on 20 April 1985.

Public schoolboy Prince Makhosetive (born 1966) became an overnight old Shirburnian when he was recalled from Sherborne School in 1983 for his coronation as King Mswati of Swaziland. He succeeded his father, King Sobhuza II, who had been absolute monarch of the southern African kingdom, a former British protectorate, for more than 60 years. The late King had dozens of wives and hundreds of children. His chosen son and heir, whilst at Sherborne, was known as Mac.

By the 1980s, keeping Sherborne's rugby tradition alive was down to a 'dedicated few', and 'the main form of recreation for Shirburnians was hockey.' Unarmed combat with rules had been replaced by the anarchy of barbarian hordes let loose with cudgels and hard balls.

The fifteenth-century Abbot's Hall, consecrated as a chapel to St John the Evangelist in 1855, had its side-chapel refurbished and rededicated to St Andrew by Bishop John Cavell, grandfather of Shirburnian Angus Craigie, on 4 March 1985. Arthur Hearne made the altar and Mrs Delma Prince provided its frontal.

The School House play in 1988 was Joe Orton's *Loot*, exposing a corrupt but untouchable police force, in the greatest work of the posthumous playwright killed by his lover, Kenneth Halliwell (who then committed suicide). There was only one straight role in the play 'though the homosexual tendencies were played down to minimise any offence.' Lyon House presented *Jonah and the Whale* with an all-male cast mostly in drag, including Toby Burnham as the most beautiful woman in Nineveh. Digby House gave us Tom Stoppard's *Albert Bridge* portraying the relationship between Andy Colville, as Albert the painter, and his canvas as the Clifton Suspension Bridge beneath his brush. James Eden helped David Rees direct a production in which would-be suicides backed off from quitting a society that 'is just about tenable'. The words controversial and stunning were applied to 'an hour and a half of extremely good theatre'.

On 25 May 1988, celebrating its centenary, Sherborne School's Cadet Corps gathered in Sherborne Park to put on a special display for Field-Marshal Lord Bramall. As General Sir Edwin Bramall he was appointed Chief of the General Staff in 1979.

An educational era ended in 1988 when Robin Donnelly Macnaghten (born 1927) retired as head-master of Sherborne School. A housemaster from Eton, he arrived in 1974, and while at Sherborne showed a disciplinarian flourish almost worthy of his former school's famous nineteenth-century master, Dr John Keate. He 'swiped' 80 boys in a single session. There had been an outbreak of co-ordinated shoplifting in Cheap Street, which galvanised Macnaghten into taking decisive action, *The Times* reported on 8 June 1988:

*Macnaghten did not match his score but he did lay into 28 of the new intake of 13 and 14-year-olds. Times will change at Sherborne in the autumn when Peter Lapping, headmaster of Shiplake, takes over. Lapping, born in India, educated in South Africa and at Lincoln College, Oxford, has a character as force-ful as it is charm-ing. He dismissed beating, succinctly, as 'out of date'.*

*Sherborne Fair with a king-sized bouncy castle towering above the Terrace.*

# Northern Town
*
## Coldharbour

Right: *Skateboarder passing Hazelwyn* (left) *and Clarence Villas* (centre and right) *on the north side of central Coldharbour.*

Below: *Lerryn* (left) *and the last of the Victorian houses north-eastwards along Coldharbour.*

Below: *The east end of Coldharbour, southwards from the junction with Bristol Road before installation of traffic lights, with the shop fronts of 1984 comprising Bryan Cooper builder, K. Rowsell butcher, Sherborne Florist, Sherborne Cycles and the Mandarin House Chinese take-away.*

## Newell & Bristol Road

Above: *The main frontage of the Crown Inn, eastwards from Newell Green, with a glimpse of Greenhill (top right).*

Right: *Walton on the west side of Bristol Road, in 2000, could boast the best garden in Sherborne.*

*The Crown Inn, in Newell, south-eastwards to the bottom curve of Greenhill.*

*Cornhill & George Street*

Above: *Barton Farm, on Kitt Hill, north-westwards towards the part of the town selected for development and expansion, from the original line of Cornhill (since incorporated into Acreman Street).*

Top: *Terraced cottages at Cornhill south-eastwards into Acreman Street (right) where the Cornhill name has now transferred to the slope below the Scot's pine trees.*

Left: *Terrace of nineteenth-century artisan cottages along the west side of George Street in a view south towards George Yard.*

# Twenty-Five

## 1990–1999

The new liberalism reached Sherborne School in 1993 when pupils were told that branching out into extra-mural activities could 'widen one's social horizon to include boys from other houses and even other years.' They received and passed its first inspections under the provisions of the Children Act. 'How far are the girls' opinions taken into account?' a prefect was asked. 'What opinions?' he answered.

One of the disappointments of the decade, for one who had been a patron for a couple of decades, was that the delicensed Black Horse Hotel, opposite the New Road junction in Oborne Road, was converted into three houses and six flats in 1994. Other key buildings were also facing a time of change including Sherborne House, which was in limbo after the departure that year of the girls of Lord Digby's School, and Sherborne Abbey where two major elements of the fabric were facing renewal.

Having the heaviest peal of eight bells in the world had taken their toll – the pun of tower captain Ross Adams – and in February 1995 they were lowered from Sherborne Abbey and taken to Nicholson Engineering at Bridport for a £32,000 overhaul and restoration. Headstocks, bearings, wheels, pulley assemblies, clappers, stays and sliders were replaced. Cast-in crown staples were removed. Ross Adams explained that they had last received attention back in 1934:

*The average weight of the eight bells is just under one ton. This combined with the fact that they are fitted with oversized headstocks and exceptionally large wheels make them extremely slow to ring – for example the average quarter peal takes about an hour to ring out and on other bells this would take only about 45 minutes. Despite this they are constantly in demand by visiting bands of ringers.*

The work to make them 'more of a matched set of eight that will enhance their international reputation' coincided with the Abbey making national headlines. Five years of ecclesiastical litigation ended in July 1995 when Salisbury Consistory Court ruled that the 1851-manufactured west window in Sherborne Abbey could be removed to a store of the Worshipful Company of Glaziers in the City of London. Designed by Augustus Pugin, at a time when he was at his busiest with the Palace of Westminster and Great Exhibition, it may well have been made by an associate, John Hayward. Pugin definitely designed the Abbey's south transept window, which was described as 'excellent' by Sir Nikolaus Pevsner, but opinions divided over the virtues or otherwise of the west window.

Its ousting was in favour of a £170,000 creation of Dorset craftsman John Hayward. Ruth Gledhill of *The Times* described him as 'a contemporary artist who has windows in St Mary-le-Bow Church in the City of London and in Dunstable Priory.' His 'Tree of Life' alternative to the work of Pugin and Hardman was in turn criticised by retired solicitor Reginald Wood for 'a ghostly green glow'.

Stronger spin of sound-bite quality came courtesy an unnamed and unknown schoolboy who had been heard to utter that one of Pugin's pink faces of 27 Old Testament prophets and patriarchs was 'like Mr Blobby'. The vicar, Revd Eric Woods, may have been 'not really aware of who Mr Blobby was' but with matching rhetoric he accompanied this image with one of red and blue discs. These, he said, had been 'likened to railway signals and traffic lights'.

The Victorian stained glass, the vicar declared, was 'really quite vulgar' and 'very commonplace'. The prolonged debate said as much about contemporary thought patterns as it did of retrospective attitudes to art. The main defender, Dr William Filmar-Sankey of the Victorian Society, counter-attacked by claiming that Pugin had an aversion to pink and insisted that there was 'no link between Mr Blobby and Pugin's window'.

The damage had been done, however, because the media delighted in continuing to compare them. In this the Consistory Court concurred, after a hearing held in the Abbey, in sight of the offending stained glass, that was held in public. 'I have to say that he had a point,' said Judge John Ellison, chancellor of the diocese of Salisbury, regarding the anecdote of the boy and his Mr Blobby allusion. The leader writer in *The Times* of 17 July 1995 pondered over 'Blobby between mullions' and enthused over the demotion of Augustus Pugin by William Morris, John Piper, Matisse and Chagall:

*Stained glass has been continually replaced by new styles or by the Blitz providing the pieces for a new kaleidoscope. Only rare buildings such as Canterbury and York have their original glass. The church at Fairford in Gloucestershire retains original fifteenth-century glass in every window. But Sherborne now has its chance to renew the mosaic of light and colour in a modern idiom. And the episode, with its shades of Ealing comedy, adds to the old art by which the people see through a glass, not darkly but with all the colours of the English sunshine.*

Sherborne House in Newland was also going through the traumas of transition. 'Progress continues on Sherborne House project,' proclaimed a Dorset County Council press release of 18 September 1994. When I went along to photograph the results in 1996 I found the 700-strong Friends of Sherborne House had enlisted the support of old Shirburnian actor Jeremy Irons and were halfway into a £1.5 million appeal. The building had been the home of Lord Digby's School for Girls since 1931.

Meanwhile, however, the more vociferous of the friends and the charity trustees of the house were clashing in the press in an embarrassingly public difference of opinion which reportedly caused the resignation of their high-profile patron. It all tended to overshadow the work being done 'to develop this important part of Sherborne's architectural heritage as a major new tourist and arts facility.' The argument over turning it into an exhibition centre was worthy of dialogue created for Victorian character actor William Macready who had lived there and brought Charles Dickens to Sherborne.

'A Dickens of a mess,' was how I summed up the situation for the new *Dorset* magazine as the once-prim lawn outside the house looked like a hay meadow on midsummer's day in 1996. It was. I suggested, 'long enough, one would imagine, for the project to have acquired, begged or borrowed a lawn-mower.' Having entertained us for so long, the endeavour eventually reached its objectives, but it was hardly surprising that I was not invited to view the splendidly restored mural by eighteenth-century Sir James Thornhill of Weymouth and Thornhill House, Stalbridge, who was 'Queen Anne's favourite artist'.

Sherborne's MP, tipped for a future Prime Minister, is Dr Oliver Letwin (born 1956) from Eton and N.M. Rothschild and Sons Limited, bankers, who took the West Dorset seat in 1997 against a strong Liberal-Democrat challenge. He soon became Shadow Home Secretary. His 1984-published study on *Ethics, Emotion and the Unity of Self* charted the way ahead for a 'philosopher politician, author and atheistic Jew'.

The decade ended with 'the best known adulterer in the country', being old Shirburnian actor Charles Collingwood, in his radio role as Brian Aldridge of 'The Archers'.

*Sherborne Abbey* (centre), *in a view north-westwards from the Slopes, in 1984.*

The Yeatman Hospital, founded by Harry Farr Yeatman in 1866, from its grounds in 1903.

## Western Town
### Hospital Lane

Above: *Abbey Grange on the east side of Hospital Lane, converted from a late-fourteenth-century monastic granary and acquired by Sherborne School in 1969, for its Headmaster's House.*

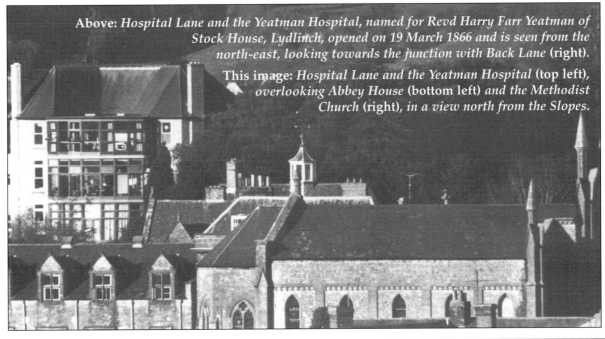

**Above:** *Hospital Lane and the Yeatman Hospital, named for Revd Harry Farr Yeatman of Stock House, Lydlinch, opened on 19 March 1866 and is seen from the north-east, looking towards the junction with Back Lane (right).*

**This image:** *Hospital Lane and the Yeatman Hospital (top left), overlooking Abbey House (bottom left) and the Methodist Church (right), in a view north from the Slopes.*

## Horsecastles

*Horsecastles Terrace, north-westwards from the Travellers' Rest* **(left, now renamed Skippers),** *from the crossroads at Horsecastles Lane.*

Below: *The great terrace of 30 matching houses in a terrace along the north side of Horsecastles (foreground), built in 1860 for silk-mill workers, in a view northwards to Half Acres and Richmond Road in 1984.*

## Bradford Road

Above: *Damping down after the blaze that damaged Sherborne School for Girls, January 1911.*

Below: *The main buildings of Sherborne School for Girls along the south side of Bradford Road, dominated by the tower of the gabled Tudor-style block (centre) that was designed by Sir Reginald Blomfield and built in 1926.*

Above: *Tower (top left) and buildings of Sherborne School for Girls from the north-west in 2000.*

Below: *Proctors, in Bradford Road, typifies early-twentieth-century villa country in Sherborne's cosy suburbia.*

## Lenthay Road

Left: *Resurrection tympanum, sculpted by James Frank Redfern, above the doorway of the Digby Mausoleum.*

Below left: *The Digby Mausoleum – incorporating a mortuary chapel – in the cemetery beside Lenthay Road.*

Below right: *West-facing front of the Digby Mausoleum which was commissioned by George Digby Wingfield Digby and designed by William Slater in 1862.*

# Postscript: The New Millennium

Sherborne's centennial celebrations – including those for the millennium – came to their climax five years later. That was the case in 1905, with Louis Napoleon Parker and his 'mother of all pageants', and is destined to be followed by another burst of cultural events in 2005. That will be the thirteenth-hundredth anniversary of the founding of Sherborne Cathedral. There are other ancient towns in Dorset but none has a distant date of such significance that comes with certainty from contemporary annals of recorded history.

The Pageant of 1905 will be followed by the Festival of Music and Drama in 2005. In place for the countdown, as vicar of Sherborne, is Canon Eric Woods who came to Sherborne Abbey after Canon Robert Willis left in 1992 – for Hereford Cathedral – and is now Dean of Canterbury. The new director of the Abbey choir, Joseph Sentence, who was appointed in 2002, has already reformed and reinvigorated what had become an endangered institution. By Christmas in 2003 he had trained 22 boys and in the process brought several young families into active participation in church and town life.

As the background to the new Sherborne sound the organ, on 'borrowed time' according to two sets of independent consultants, has been earmarked for its first complete rebuilding since installation in the 1850s. In the interregnum – making what head verger Keith Batten describes as 'its own good sound' – is an electronic organ which made its service debut in December 2003.

Much angst has flowed from water mains and cobbles. Between them they have achieved months of traffic gridlock while the Victorian infrastructure is being repaired and replaced. Lead pipes are either being removed or lined with benign coatings. Cobbled paving, or granite stonesetts to be more precise, have made their return for the purposes of traffic calming with that unique heritage look. This, in the process, has enraged an unlikely consortium of aggrieved users from pram-pushers and the disabled through to shopkeepers and white-van drivers. Keith Batten, chatting in the vestry at the Abbey, summed up current controversies for me:

*A lot of people would like to leave the town as it is, but you can't. It has to function as a community rather than a collection of museum exhibits. Because of the work that is going on, they say that at the moment we have as many traffic lights in Sherborne as there are roundabouts in Basingstoke, but all that will sort itself out. The bigger issue, where people get really angry, is over new housing developments. Unless these happen young people will not be able to afford to buy property to stay in their own home town.*

This century will also notch up the first half-millennium of Sherborne School. That it is an on-going process is shown by the following potted paragraphs summing up the lives of a few former pupils of Sherborne School and its governors who were receiving mentions – some of them posthumously – in newspapers and books during the time that the current title was being compiled. There will be a much more cosmopolitan feel to future registers as international enrolments proceed apace. There has been no attempt here at selecting out the odd black sheep from amongst last century's intake but none grabbed headlines. It is very much a personal selection.

Alan Lennox-Boyd, 1st Viscount Boyd (1904–83), a governor of Sherborne School from 1962, was a former Colonial Secretary. Sir Alan Campbell (born 1919), an old Shirburnian diplomat OS diplomat, was a governor from 1973. Sir Geoffrey Chandler (born 1922), another old Shirburnian, was Director-General of the National Economic Development Office.

Major General Patrick Cordingley (born 1944), an old Shirburnian, commanded the 7th Armoured Brigade in the first Gulf War of 1991. Lieutenant-Colonel Sir Thomas Devitt (1902–95), old Shirburnian and Seaforth Highlander, a shipbroker by profession, was a governor of Sherborne School from 1967 to 1975. Air Commodore Peter Langloh Donkin (born 1913), another Shirburnian, went from being a wartime Wing Commander to flying the 'desk of danger' as Air Attaché in Moscow at the height of the Cold War.

Jeremy Irons (born 1948), an old Shirburnian actor, came to fame co-starring with Meryl Streep in the film of John Fowles' novel *The French Lieutenant's Woman*. Sir Christopher Lawrence-Jones (born 1940) became the Shirburnian expert on industrial medicine. Sir Arthur Norman (born 1933) chaired the World Wildlife Fund and the governors of Sherborne School. Sir Rodney Pasley (1899–1982), an old Shirburnian historian, brought his famous ancestor to life by publishing the *Private Sea Journals of Admiral Sir Thomas Pasley*, from 1778 to 1782.

Sir Alastair Pilkington (1920–95) was the old Shirburnian chairman of Pilkington Brothers, the country's principal glass manufacturers. General Sir Roy Redgrave (born 1925), old Shirburnian Commandant of the Royal Armoured Corps Centre at Bovington and Lulworth in Dorset, left Dorset to become British Commandant in Berlin. Sir George Truscott (born 1919) became a distinguished old Shirburnian businessman. The Honourable Sir Henry Tucker (1903–86) was the old Shirburnian Government Leader in Bermuda. Sir Peter Watkin Williams (born 1911) was an old Shirburnian Chief Justice, across the British Empire from St Helena to Swaziland, and President of Court of Appeal from 1961 to 1965. Professor Sir Robert Williams (born 1916) became the eminent old Shirburnian pathologist and director of the Public Health Laboratory Service.

As a result of such achievements at the end of the learning stream, Sherborne's position is secure, among those rare places that have entered the national psyche.

# Subscribers

❧

Mrs Sheila Adams, Sherborne
Florence R. Alexander, Sherborne Girls School, Dorset
Lady M.L. Alexander, Sherborne, Dorset
Robin, Bernie, Jonathan and James Ansell, Sherborne, Dorset
Bill Bennette, Rose Leigh, Dorset
Hibbert A.H. Binney, Sherborne, Dorset
Barry Brock, Sherborne, Dorset
Edward Brock, Tooting, London
Rosalind Brock, Windlesham, Surrey
J.W. and B.K. Bunker
Mr Michael Butler, Templecombe
John Clarke, Sherborne, Dorset
Michael Clarke, Sherborne, Dorset
Richard C. Cockram, Sherborne, Dorset
Mrs Eileen Margorie Dash, Sherborne, Dorset
Miss Margaret Dash, Sherborne, Dorset
Betty Dewberry (née Hamblin), Sherborne, Dorset
Adrian Dodge, Cheap Street, Sherborne
Dorset County Council, Dorchester Library
Dorset County Council, Gillingham Library
Dorset County Council, Shaftesbury Library
Dorset County Council, Stalbridge Library
Dorset County Council, Sherborne Library
Mr Alan Drew, Sherborne, Dorset
Dyne Drewett, Sherborne, Dorset
James Earle, Sherborne, Dorset
Michael and Ann Evans, Chetnole, Dorset
Michael J. Evans, Yeovil, Somerset
Major and Mrs A.W. Floyd-Jewell
David George Gay, Sherborne, Dorset
John Goodden, Compton House, Over Compton, Sherborne
Michael Goodden, Compton House, Over Compton, Sherborne
Robert and Rosemary Goodden, Compton House, Over Compton
Sally Goodden, Compton House, Over Compton, Sherborne
Olive E. Goodwin, Sherborne, Dorset
Ken and Dee Gosling, North Cheriton, Somerset
Eileen J. Guppy, Sherborne, Dorset
Karen Haig-Brown, Sherborne, Dorset

Mr Dave Hallett, Yeovil, Somerset
G. and C. Harvey, Sherborne
Alan S. Hemmings, Sherborne
Jean and Jonathan Hill,
Shelagh Hill, Sherborne
Keith Ireland, Sherborne, Dorset
Rene Keep, Sherborne, Dorset
Mrs Margaret Lane, Newland, Sherborne
Kenneth R. Lumb, Sherborne
Nesta McDonald, Sherborne, Dorset
W.G. Monnery, Sherborne
Brian F. Morey, Sherborne, Dorset
Simon J. Newcombe, Sherborne, Dorset
George and Rita Newman, Sherborne, Dorset
Gwen Newman, Auweston
Randolph Oliver, Champion Ploughman, Dorset
Adrian Park, Milborne Port, Sherborne
Di Park, Newland, Sherborne
Alex Pay, Sherborne, Dorset
Mary and Graham Pay, Sherborne, Dorset
Vicki Pay, Sherborne, Dorset
Dr R.G. Penn, Sherborne, Dorset
C.P.C. and J.H. Pettit, Shenington, Oxfordshire
David J. Phillips, Longburton, Dorset
R. Pountain, Sherborne, Dorset
Harrison E. Pow-Jones
Russell M. Pow-Jones
Ian and Jean Raby, formerly of Sherborne
Michael and Jean Rawlinson, Lyn Cottage, Hound Street, Sherborne
F.W.B. Saunders, Sherborne
Sherborne Museum Association, Church Lane, Sherborne
Mr and Mrs Frank Skinner, Sherborne, Dorset
David and Patsy Spicer
John and Vera Stranger, Milborne Port
Charles and Jane Sweet, Sherborne, Dorset
Champion Thomas, Sherborne, Dorset
Glennis Thomas, Sherborne, Dorset
Mr and Mrs B. Todd, Sherborne, Dorset
Anne Turberville-Smith, Sherborne
Mrs Jane Turner, Fir Cottage, Coldharbour, Sherborne
John F.W. Walling, Newton Abbot, Devon
Jennie Ward
Brus Watters, Sherborne
Julia C. Welland, Sherborne, Dorset
Stanley and Dee Westoll, Hermitage, Dorset
Rosie Wheeler, Stoke Trister, Somerset
Jenny Whitemoore, Sherborne, Dorset
K.P. Wightman, Sherborne, Dorset
Canon Eric Woods, Sherborne Abbey

## *Community Histories*

The Book of Addiscombe • Canning and Clyde Road Residents Association and Friends
The Book of Addiscombe, Vol. II • Canning and Clyde Road Residents Association and Friends
The Book of Ashburton • Stuart Hands and Pete Webb
The Book of Axminster with Kilmington • Les Berry
and Gerald Gosling
The Book of Bampton • Caroline Seward
The Book of Barnstaple • Avril Stone
The Book of Barnstaple, Vol. II • Avril Stone
The Book of The Bedwyns • Bedwyn History Society
The Book of Bickington • Stuart Hands
Blandford Forum: A Millennium Portrait • Blandford Forum
Town Council
The Book of Boscastle • Rod and Anne Knight
The Book of Bramford • Bramford Local History Group
The Book of Breage & Germoe • Stephen Polglase
The Book of Bridestowe • D. Richard Cann
The Book of Bridport • Rodney Legg
The Book of Brixham • Frank Pearce
The Book of Buckfastleigh • Sandra Coleman
The Book of Buckland Monachorum & Yelverton • Pauline Hamilton-Leggett
The Book of Carharrack • Carharrack Old
Cornwall Society
The Book of Carshalton • Stella Wilks and Gordon Rookledge
The Parish Book of Cerne Abbas • Vivian and
Patricia Vale
The Book of Chagford • Iain Rice
The Book of Chapel-en-le-Frith • Mike Smith
The Book of Chittlehamholt with
Warkleigh & Satterleigh • Richard Lethbridge
The Book of Chittlehampton • Various
The Book of Colney Heath • Bryan Lilley
The Book of Constantine • Moore and Trethowan
The Book of Cornwood and Lutton • Compiled by
the People of the Parish
The Book of Crediton • John Heal
The Book of Creech St Michael • June Small
The Book of Cullompton • Compiled by the People
of the Parish
The Book of Dawlish • Frank Pearce
The Book of Dulverton, Brushford,
Bury & Exebridge • Dulverton and District Civic Society
The Book of Dunster • Hilary Binding
The Book of Easton • Easton Village History Project
The Book of Edale • Gordon Miller
The Ellacombe Book • Sydney R. Langmead
The Book of Exmouth • W.H. Pascoe
The Book of Grampound with Creed • Bane and Oliver
The Book of Gosport • Lesley Burton and
Brian Musselwhite
The Book of Hayling Island & Langstone • Peter Rogers
The Book of Helston • Jenkin with Carter
The Book of Hemyock • Clist and Dracott

*The Book of Herne Hill* • Patricia Jenkyns
*The Book of Hethersett* • Hethersett Society
Research Group
*The Book of High Bickington* • Avril Stone
*The Book of Ilsington* • Dick Wills
*The Book of Kingskerswell* • Carsewella Local
History Group
*The Book of Lamerton* • Ann Cole and Friends
*Lanner, A Cornish Mining Parish* • Sharron
Schwartz and Roger Parker
*The Book of Leigh & Bransford* • Malcolm Scott
*The Book of Litcham with Lexham & Mileham* • Litcham Historical and Amenity Society
*The Book of Loddiswell* • Loddiswell Parish
History Group
*The New Book of Lostwithiel* • Barbara Fraser
*The Book of Lulworth* • Rodney Legg
*The Book of Lustleigh* • Joe Crowdy
*The Book of Lydford* • Compiled by Barbara Weeks
*The Book of Lyme Regis* • Rodney Legg
*The Book of Manaton* • Compiled by the People
of the Parish
*The Book of Markyate* • Markyate Local History Society
*The Book of Mawnan* • Mawnan Local History Group
*The Book of Meavy* • Pauline Hemery
*The Book of Mere* • Dr David Longbourne
*The Book of Minehead with Alcombe* • Binding and Stevens
*The Book of Monks Orchard and Eden Park* • Ian Muir and Pat Manning
*The Book of Morchard Bishop* • Jeff Kingaby
*The Book of Mylor* • Mylor Local History Group
*The Book of Narborough* • Narborough Local
History Society
*The Book of Newdigate* • John Callcut
*The Book of Newtown* • Keir Foss
*The Book of Nidderdale* • Nidderdale Museum Society
*The Book of Northlew with Ashbury* • Northlew
History Group
*The Book of North Newton* • J.C. and K.C. Robins
*The Book of North Tawton* • Baker, Hoare and Shields
*The Book of Nynehead* • Nynehead & District
History Society
*The Book of Okehampton* • Roy and Ursula Radford
*The Book of Ottery St Mary* • Gerald Gosling and
Peter Harris
*The Book of Paignton* • Frank Pearce
*The Book of Penge, Anerley & Crystal Palace* •
Peter Abbott
*The Book of Peter Tavy with Cudlipptown* • Peter Tavy Heritage Group
*The Book of Pimperne* • Jean Coull
*The Book of Plymtree* • Tony Eames
*The Book of Porlock* • Dennis Corner
*Postbridge – The Heart of Dartmoor* • Reg Bellamy
*The Book of Priddy* • Albert Thompson
*The Book of Princetown* • Dr Gardner-Thorpe
*The Book of Probus* • Alan Kent and Danny Merrifield

For details of any of the above titles or if you are
interested in writing your own history, please contact:
Commissioning Editor, Community Histories, Halsgrove House,
Lower Moor Way, Tiverton, Devon EX16 6SS, England;
email: katyc@halsgrove.com